# HIDDEN SORROW, LASTING JOY

## The Forgotten Women of the Persecuted Church

# Hidden Sorrow, Lasting Joy

## THE FORGOTTEN WOMEN OF THE PERSECUTED CHURCH

### ANNEKE COMPANJEN

TYNDALE HOUSE PUBLISHERS, INC., WHEATON, ILLINOIS

Visit Tyndale's exciting Web site at www.tyndale.com

*Hidden Sorrow, Lasting Joy: The Forgotten Women of the Persecuted Church*

Copyright © 2001 by Open Doors International, Inc. All rights reserved.

Cover photograph copyright © 2001 by Jed Share/Stone. All rights reserved.

Author photograph copyright © 2001 by Turville Photography. All rights reserved.

Edited by Jeremy P. Taylor and Dan Lins

Designed by Dean H. Renninger

Scripture quotations are taken from the Holy Bible, New International Version®. NIV®. Copyright © 1973, 1978, 1984 by International Bible Society. Used by permission of Zondervan Publishing House. All rights reserved.

---

**Library of Congress Cataloging-in-Publication Data**

Companjen, Anneke.
  Hidden sorrow, lasting joy / Anneke Companjen.
    p. cm.
  ISBN 0-8423-4320-2 (sc)
   1. Persecution—History—20th century. 2. Political prisoners' spouses—Biography. 3. Christian women—
Biography. I. Title.
BR1608.5 .C66 2001
272'.9'0922—dc21
[B]
                                           2001027330

---

Printed in the United States of America

05  04  03  02  01
8    7    6    5    4    3    2

# DEDICATION

This book is lovingly dedicated to the memory of Margie Johnson, my friend and fellow prayer partner for the Suffering Church, who died before this book could be published. It is my prayer that the following stories will be used to raise up more women like Margie:

Women who give
Women who minister
Women who pray

# CONTENTS

# ACKNOWLEDGMENTS

This book could not have been written without the help and support of others. First of all, I am deeply indebted to the wives who allowed me to tell their stories. I pray that their burdens will become lighter because their hidden sorrows have been made known in this book.

Our Open Doors program directors have been of invaluable help, providing me with the necessary information, checking the manuscript for correctness, and always bearing in mind the security of the women about whom I have written.

Alan Hall, the Open Doors vice president of Development, has done a lot of work behind the scenes. His sound advice, as well as that of board members Sealy Yates and Al Janssen, was greatly appreciated.

Alex Buchan allowed me to include the chapter he wrote about Ah Ju. Luke and Angie Yeghnazar were a valuable resource regarding the situation of the Iranian widows. Lynn Muelle was very helpful to me in capturing the story of Rosa O'Caldo.

I am greatly indebted to Lela Gilbert, who did more than just edit the original manuscript. She became my teacher and my editor as she put my thoughts into much better words.

I am very grateful to Brother Andrew for his willingness to contribute to this book. His influence on my life has been profound.

And last but definitely not least there is Johan, my dear husband, who was willing to put up with an absentminded wife for over a year. Without his never-ending encouragement and faith in this project, I would have given up long ago.

*Anneke Companjen*
*Harderwijk, Holland—June 1, 2000*

# A Book from the Heart

*Speak up for those who cannot speak for themselves, for the
rights of all who are destitute. Speak up and judge fairly;
defend the rights of the poor and needy.*
*Proverbs 31:8-9*

It was Sunday evening in Harderwijk, my Dutch hometown. My
husband, Johan, was away on an extended trip, one of many that
he made throughout the year. It would be several weeks before he
was home again.

I heard muffled giggles coming from upstairs as my three children—who were supposed to be sleeping—shared another joke. I sti-
fled my annoyance, knowing that sooner or later they would doze
off. I had managed to give them an evening meal, supervise their
bath time, tell them a story, and pray with them before switching off
the light and heading downstairs. Now there was only the washing
up to do, and I would be free for the evening.

Right then I realized how weary I was. *I might as well have an early
night myself,* I thought as I tackled the stack of dirty dishes.

Once my chores were finished, I settled into bed and closed
my eyes. But sleep eluded me that night, and gradually it dawned on
me that I was more than tired. I was lonely and depressed.

*If only Johan were home,* I thought. Talking to my husband often
helped me see things from the right perspective. But Johan was half
a world away in Australia. It wasn't the first time he'd been gone for
weeks at a time that year, and I knew it wouldn't be the last.[1] As the
minutes ticked by, I began to wonder if my future would consist of

---

[1] For some thoughts on these separations written by a dear friend of ours, please read
the Afterword by Brother Andrew

nothing more than cleaning house, washing dishes, and caring for children while Johan traveled the world.

Along with all my other unpleasant feelings, I felt ashamed of myself. Many women I knew or had read about had endured much more than I was going through. I'd heard of pastor's wives who were separated from their husbands for years at a time because of imprisonment. I knew about women whose husbands had been murdered because of their Christian work; mothers whose handsome, gifted sons had been shot down in the prime of life for their faith. These women would suffer for a lifetime. Their pain wouldn't vanish—like mine—in just a couple more weeks.

As the tide of my emotions finally began to ebb, I heard the Lord's still, small voice, speaking to my heart:

*Through what you are experiencing now, you will one day be able to help other women. I am allowing you to feel this pain so you will be able to understand and empathize with them.*

Not quite sure what the words meant, I finally drifted off to sleep.

In the 1990s the topic of the persecution of Christians became well known in the United States. Led by *The New York Times,* major newspapers wrote stories about the subject. In the United States Congress, legislation was passed to help control it. Christian leaders and organizations spoke out and demanded a response. After decades of apathy, the Western church finally began to awaken to the clear and present danger faced by 200 million Christian brothers and sisters around the world.

But to those of us at work in the world on behalf of the gospel, the persecution of Christians was not a new problem.

In the late 1960s and 1970s we were shocked to hear about Pastor Richard Wurmbrand's experiences in a Romanian prison. Brother Andrew often held us spellbound as he shared about his trips to take Bibles into Eastern Europe. The suffering of Russian Christians became better and better known as several Russian Baptist brothers found refuge in Germany. As a result, many Christians have long been active in restricted countries, helping to provide the believers there with Bibles, encouragement, and support.

My husband, Johan, was one of them, and during the years I stayed at home to look after our children, he kept me well informed. More recently, I have had the privilege of sharing in several of his travels, friendships, and commitments. I have become more and more aware of the tragic toll that persecution takes on believers. Christian husbands—many of them pastors and church leaders—have been abused, imprisoned, and sometimes martyred.

When I heard about what happened to K'Sup Nri, whose story you'll read first, I realized that the courageous wives of these men are often overlooked and forgotten. And I began to understand the Lord's long-ago message to my heart: *I am allowing you to feel this pain so you will be able to understand and empathize with them.*

These women have struggled with painful separation, loss, and uncertainty. They have been ostracized by their culture, left alone to care for fatherless children, and subjected to crushing poverty. Their faith has been stretched to the limit, and yet they have rarely been the subjects of prayer campaigns or human-rights projects. At a time when women's rights have become a popular cause, these women's needs have remained virtually unknown.

Hidden Sorrow, *Lasting Joy* is a tribute to such forgotten women. It is the story of twenty women of courage and endurance, and that story's message to women and men in the West. Some of their names have been changed, and some details of their experiences have been modified because of security concerns. Some of the stories do not have happy endings. But all of them are true.

The women of the Suffering Church are not superwomen. Neither are their husbands spiritual supermen. Some seem stronger than others, but all of them have their weak moments. Some remain standing in the midst of great pressure. Others give in to temptation.

One chapter of this book had to be omitted because—between writing and publication—a wife left her family during her husband's imprisonment and moved in with another man. To protect her husband and family, it seemed wise not to include their story. But I continue to hurt and to pray for this woman and her family. And they are not the only ones.

In the pages that follow, you will read of women from countries all around the world. Most of them have known tremendous sorrow. Some of them continue to wrestle with rejection, poverty, shame, and constant harassment by the authorities. They battle their own doubts, fears, and anger. Most have made the choice to accept their pain and use it to be a blessing to others.

But as you read, I think you will see that the story of the Suffering Church is not a negative tale as is sometimes thought. It is often a story of great rejoicing in the midst of affliction, of unexplainable peace in the midst of pain. It is about seasons of sorrow that must be hidden, and about joy that will last eternally.

It is for these reasons I have written. It is my prayer that God will use this book to help us all be better colaborers with Christ. I hope that we will remember the women of the Suffering Church in our prayers, support them through our churches, and provide for them in practical ways whenever possible. Perhaps even more, I pray that their courage, their faithfulness, and their commitment to Christ will forever change our lives.

As you meet them, I hope you will catch a glimpse of their personalities, their courage, and the faith that sustains them. These are women with the same longings, desires, and fears as you and I. They are mothers, daughters, sisters, and aunts. Some are young, some are old; others are aging too quickly for their years. Some are rich in hope; others contend with relentless depression. Above all else, they very much need our prayers. When you pray for their husbands in prison, will you also pray for them, too? Let's ask God to transform their sorrow, which must remain hidden today, into lasting joy and peace.

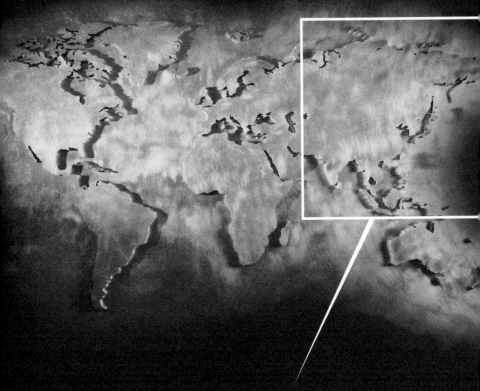

ASIA

# K'SUP NRI

## TRAGIC ENDING, NEW BEGINNING

I will never forget her face. Sweet and childlike, K'Sup Nri seemed fragile, even at first glance. Her smile was a little shy; her manner gentle. K'Sup Nri's beauty personified many of the qualities that endeared me to her people. I couldn't have imagined, the sunny afternoon we met, the tragedy that awaited her.

CHAPTER I

The air was crisp, and the sun shone that January day in 1973. My infant son, Mark, had just awakened from his nap, and Marjan, his older sister, was getting restless. "I think you two would be happier if we all took a nice walk," I informed them. And out we went.

Record my lament; list my tears on your scroll—are they not in your record?

*Psalm 56:8*

Less than a month before, our family had packed up, left Holland, and arrived in the beautiful city of Dalat, located in the central highlands of Vietnam. As missionaries serving with the Christian and Missionary Alliance (CAMA) our first task was to try to master the difficult Vietnamese language. My husband, Johan, had already started language study. Because Mark was just a month old when we arrived, I was not yet able to attend school. But I was eager to learn Vietnamese, so I started taking lessons at home with a private tutor and tried to practice whenever I got the chance.

Life was delightful for us those first weeks in Vietnam. During our Bible-college years in England, Johan and I had lived with twelve boys in a school residence. Afterward, we had stayed with our parents while making preparations to go overseas. For the first time since our wedding in 1970, we had a house all to ourselves. It was like a dream come true.

And we couldn't have imagined a more picturesque place to live. Dalat was a scenic mountain resort that was once the home of

3

Dalat School, where missionary kids from all over southeast Asia had lived and studied. The Vietnam War forced the school to relocate to Malaysia, and the campus, now called Villa Alliance, was a conference center. We had made our home in one of the holiday cottages. The climate was wonderful—much cooler than the sweltering coastal plains—and the view of the mountainous countryside was breathtaking.

As soon as the children and I went outside that day, a friendly group of neighboring children appeared. Their older sister was taking care of them, and my two little blonds quickly caught their attention. Like typical kids, they skipped and chattered and laughed as we all made our way around the compound.

We were returning to our house when a tribal woman came walking toward us. It was the first time I met K'Sup Nri.

I was immediately aware of her natural poise and charm. Her long black skirt, which wrapped gracefully around her waist, told me that she belonged to one of the many ethnic minority groups of the Vietnamese highlands. K'Sup Nri was instantly attracted to my children, and she and I began to communicate. I was still learning the most basic Vietnamese words, so we relied heavily on hand motions. Not many words were needed for me to understand that she was expecting her first baby and that she was ecstatic about it.

Later on, our missionary colleagues told me more about her. She and her husband, "Dieu," belonged to the Stieng, a primitive tribe who lived in dense jungle among the rolling rubber plantations northwest of Saigon, along the Cambodian border. They came from the area around An Loc, the provincial capital. Heavy fighting had caused them and many of their ethnic minority group to flee; a resettlement camp had been set up for the refugees about an hour's drive from Dalat.

Besides helping Ralph and Lorraine Hauper, Wycliffe missionaries who were translating the Bible into the Stieng vernacular, K'Sup Nri worked with her husband, the young pastor of the newly-converted Stieng Christians. At that time their tribe was experiencing an exciting spiritual revival, and they were really excited about the way the Lord was using them.

The living conditions in the couple's resettlement camp were far from good, especially during the rainy season. When monsoons turned the roads into sticky red mud, only four-wheel drive vehicles could reach the rows of tents. But when it wasn't raining, Johan and I loved nothing more than loading up our Jeep on Sunday mornings and worshiping with the Stieng people. Never mind the drive with two very small children, this was what we had come to Vietnam for—to see the gospel do its transforming work in the lives of men and women.

After one particular worship service, we all trailed into the woods to attend a baptismal meeting. Dieu, the only Stieng pastor at the time, baptized several new believers. I can still picture Dieu standing in that stream, up to his knees in water, his face shining in the hot sun. And K'Sup Nri was a portrait of happiness as she watched her husband perform the baptism. Her lovely smile radiated joy and love toward him and their people. Great joy filled our hearts, too. Back home in Holland, our youth group had often sung, "All over the world, the Spirit is moving." Now with our own eyes we were seeing that the words of the song were true.

After returning from the baptism, we enjoyed chicken curry and lively conversation in the fellowship's makeshift, army-green refugee tent. Curious locals crowded around to examine the strange-looking foreigners. The thick, blond hair on Johan's arms was a great attraction, and everyone seemed to want to pinch our babies' white skin. Even though we didn't especially enjoy being such a novelty, we knew that it was just one more aspect of living in Vietnam. And what we were experiencing was well worth our long journey—the Lord was clearly at work among these people. What better incentive to help us face another week of language study?

Weeks later, after we finished our language training, we were assigned to work in the coastal town of Quinhon. There we continued to hear good things about the Stieng people and the mighty work that God was doing in their lives. But it wasn't long before a major interruption distracted us from K'Sup Nri, Dieu, and our other Vietnamese friends. We had been in Vietnam for less than two and a half years, falling in love with the people and sharing in their spiritual joys and sorrows. Now we were forced to rivet our attention on our own predicament.

## An Unwelcome Interruption

The Communist takeover in 1975 caught virtually all the Western missionaries in Vietnam by surprise. While our family was attending a regional conference in Danang, in the northern part of South Vietnam, a Communist attack was suddenly launched from the North. This campaign would eventually lead the Communist troops to victory.

First we heard that five CAMA missionaries and a family in the highland city of Banmethuot working with Wycliffe Bible Translators had been captured. After a few days all radio contact with them was lost.[2]

Then, even more ominous for us, we heard that Quinhon, where we were living, was no longer safe. After some hasty discussions, we decided that Johan should return alone to pick up a few of our possessions, pay the rent and the household helper, and then return to Danang. The children and I would stay behind.

While Johan was in Quinhon, the situation in Vietnam rapidly deteriorated. He was informed that it was impossible for him to get back to us in Danang. In fact, for a time he was stranded in Quinhon. After many stressful hours in the Quinhon airport, an Air America pilot came to his rescue and flew him to Saigon.

Meanwhile, I remained in Danang with Mark and Marjan. While I waited for word about Johan, two CAMA mission leaders arrived in Saigon from the United States. They ordered all of the missionaries associated with CAMA to evacuate to Saigon. Seven years earlier, during the Tet offensive of 1968, six of our missionaries had been killed in Banmethuot.[3] The organization did not want to risk any more lives.

How would I ever get our children and myself to Saigon? Danang was full of refugees, and everybody was trying to get to the same place. I felt frightened and alone, longing for Johan to return and walk through this frightening experience with me. One sleepless night, after much tossing and turning, I wearily sat up in

---

[2] The full story of these missionaries has been told by James and Marti Hefley in their book *Prisoners of Hope* (Harrisburg, Pa.: Christian Publications Inc.).

[3] James C. Hefley, *By Life or by Death* (Grand Rapids, Mich.: Zondervan, 1969).

bed and picked up a book that was lying on my bedroom table. When I opened it, the first words I read were "I will provide!" Tears stung my eyes. I recognized God's voice, and peace settled upon me like a warm blanket. At last I slept.

A couple of days later the children and I were finally able to board a plane to Saigon. An hour later we found ourselves in the arms of my overjoyed husband. Johan had been waiting night and day at the airport. He had met every plane arriving from Danang to see if we were on it. At last we all were together again.

After a week in Saigon we were given orders to leave Vietnam. We were heartsick at the news, but there was nothing we could do. In consultation with the leaders of the Evangelical Church of Vietnam (the Tin Lanh church), CAMA's leadership had decided that it would be better for everyone concerned if all the Western missionaries left the country. The last thing we wanted to do was jeopardize the lives of the pastors and other Christians we had worked with, so we did as we were told. Besides, families with small children were more a bother than a blessing at such a time.

So, after many emotional good-byes, we found ourselves back home in Holland. Dressed in summer clothes and sandals, we arrived at Schiphol airport in freezing winter weather. Our families, whom we had been able to call just before leaving Saigon, were thrilled to see us. But our hearts were heavy. Our lifelong dream of a missionary career seemed to have ended, abruptly and perhaps forever.

It had especially hurt us to leave our Vietnamese brothers and sisters behind. What would happen to them? Sometimes K'Sup Nri's radiant smile crossed my mind, and when I thought about her I prayed, wondering about her husband and her new baby. The history of Christian suffering in Communist countries like Russia and China, did not promise a rosy future for the believers we had left behind in Vietnam.

In July 1975 our sense of foreboding about the fate of the Vietnamese church proved all too accurate. We heard reports that, along with several other pastors, Dieu had been arrested. Before long the reports were verified.

Little by little facts trickled out. For over a year Dieu had been kept in solitary confinement, his legs immobilized in stocks. Then, in April 1977 he was transported to a prison in the north of the country, where he remained for eleven years.

Meanwhile, the Stieng refugee camp near Bao Loc had been demolished, and the residents were forced to return to their native villages. Fortunately, a small group of Stieng young people were able to flee to Denmark. They kept us informed whenever there was any news about Dieu. Occasionally someone who had been imprisoned with him was released and provided an update. We were grateful to hear that Dieu continued to serve the Lord in his "reeducation camp." In fact, after his release we learned that he had led forty-four of his fellow prisoners to Christ and had baptized thirty-two of them in the woods during their lunch breaks.

## DESPAIR, DECEPTION, AND DEATH

Before our sudden departure, the Lord seemed to be telling us that we should not give up on Vietnam, even though it would soon become a "closed" country. After a few months of looking into other options in Holland and praying for guidance, Johan joined Open Doors with Brother Andrew. Before long, Johan was traveling around the world with Brother Andrew, sharing the needs of the Suffering Church with churches in the West. He challenged people to pray for those who had been imprisoned for their Christian faith. Brother Andrew always became much more interested in a country after its doors were closed to conventional missionary service. Such countries were destinations where no one else dared to go. In 1975 Vietnam fit that category.

Since Vietnam was so close to Johan's heart, he never failed to share the needs of the Christians in Vietnam. Prayer, we were all convinced, was what the Christians in that country needed—especially those in prison. So we prayed for Dieu and many others like him, but none of us knew what was happening to his young wife and their two little children.

When we finally did hear, it was too late.

Once Dieu and his brother were led away as captives, K'Sup Nri and her son were sent back to the village where she was born.

And not long after Dieu's incarceration began, K'Sup Nri gave birth to their second child, a beautiful little girl.

K'Sup Nri lived with her parents, but her loneliness was overwhelming. Her childlike appearance was no illusion. She had been a teenage bride—not much more than a child when she and Dieu had married—and she had always relied heavily upon her strong, capable husband. Now he was gone. To make matters worse, K'Sup Nri had virtually no spiritual support. All the Stieng churches were closed, and the Christians were scattered and forbidden to meet.

For years K'Sup Nri had to work very hard in the fields to provide food for her little ones. Life was incredibly hard. She longed for her husband. Where was he? Was he still alive? How were his captors treating him? No word or letter ever came. She wanted to visit him, but visits to prisoners—even by their wives—were not permitted. K'Sup Nri was crushed.

All the while, Communist cadres were pressuring K'Sup Nri and other Christians to give up their faith. Confused and isolated, the young woman would lie awake at night, remembering the past and worrying about the future.

K'Sup Nri's memories carried her back to the happier times she and her beloved husband had shared in Bao Loc. She envisioned the wonderful gatherings when all the Christians sang praises to God together and hoped to recapture some of the lyrics that had once lifted her heart. She tried to recollect the sound of her husband's voice as he explained passages from the Bible or prayed with her. In reality, she could not even remember his face very well.

In the tribal churches all the Christians would often pray out loud together. Sound would then fill the building like a sweet perfume rising to the Lord. Now all K'Sup Nri could hear when she prayed was her own voice. How she wished her husband were there to help her understand what was happening. She had learned from him that God was almighty, always able and willing to help. Where was Dieu's God now? She knew she needed help, but who could she turn to? The missionaries were gone. The tribal Christians were spread out all over the region. Who could possibly understand what she was going through?

As the children grew, they began to ask about their father. She tried to explain what had happened to him, but to her children, Dieu was a stranger, a character in an oft-repeated story. K'Sup Nri prayed persistently, but her prayers seemed to go nowhere. Then, after years of uncertainty, her worst fears were realized. Authorities came to her home and informed her that her husband had died in prison.

From that moment on K'Sup Nri's emotional life fell apart. It had been seven years since her husband had been taken away, and her sense of isolation was almost unbearable. Now that she had received word of his death, the very foundations of K'Sup Nri's life were fractured.

All that she had believed in had failed her. She had trusted God with a child's faith to keep her husband alive, but her prayers had been denied. She had tried to instill a love for Dieu in his children's hearts, but how could they love someone they didn't know? She had worked night and day to keep her family fed and sheltered, and her body ached as deeply as her mind and spirit.

"God, I need a husband!" she cried out. "I can't go on like this!"

Grief and spiritual confusion overwhelmed K'Sup Nri. Her faith had eroded into doubt; her doubt had become despair. And at this very time, when she couldn't have been more vulnerable, a young Communist officer entered the scene. He was about her age, and he was attracted to her beauty. He befriended K'Sup Nri, he listened to her, he expressed his concern. Understandably, she responded to him.

Of course the young Communist was not a Christian, and he was nothing like Dieu in any other way. But he was interested in her, and perhaps, she told herself, he was the answer to her many prayers for help. For a few months she resisted a serious relationship. She still felt emotionally attached to her children's father, but what good was that? At one time she would have asked God for wisdom, but her broken heart told her that God wouldn't answer anyway. So eventually, when the officer asked her to marry him, K'Sup Nri overcame her reluctance and gave in. At least now, she thought, she and her children would be taken care of, and she would once again have a strong shoulder to lean on. Before long the two were married.

For a little while life seemed good. K'Sup Nri's exhausting efforts to survive were relieved. Gradually she began to enjoy life again, even learning to laugh with her children once more. Then, a few months after the wedding, a neighbor came to visit, bringing along a strange rumor.

A prisoner who had been recently released was telling people that Dieu had not died after all. His brother Men was the one who had passed away. Trembling with fear, K'Sup Nri started asking questions of anyone and everyone who might know something about her first husband. The more she inquired, the more certain she was that the rumor was true. Finally, she heard for herself confirmation from the man who had been released from prison just a short time before. Yes, he assured her, Dieu was still alive, faithfully serving the Lord in his place of incarceration.

K'Sup Nri's desperation was indescribable. Regret and remorse gripped her with icy hands; hopelessness began to strangle her. To her horror, she realized that she had been lied to—the Communist authorities had intentionally deceived her. *How could I have been such a fool?* she asked herself mercilessly. Even worse, she began to suspect—and not without reason—that the authorities had also engineered her marriage to the young officer. It had all been part of their plot to destroy her husband's life and marriage. They had succeeded, and in K'Sup Nri's view, there was no one to blame but herself.

After so many years of overpowering struggle of every kind—physical, mental and spiritual—K'Sup Nri now found herself utterly without reason to live. She simply could not find the strength to face the future. By that time her faith had grown too weak to save her. Her despair condemned her. One desperate night, unable to face another day, she poisoned herself. She was found dead the next morning.

## IF ONLY WE HAD KNOWN

For weeks after I heard the tragic end of K'Sup Nri's story, I searched my soul. I couldn't stop thinking about this beautiful young woman—my friend, my fellow servant of Jesus. And I felt guilty. Had I prayed for her enough? What would have happened if Christians all over the world had prayed for her as fervently as they had prayed for her husband? Johan and others had faithfully asked for prayers for Dieu, but no one knew about K'Sup Nri's circumstances until after the worst had happened. Might she have been helped if only we had known of her struggle and interceded on her behalf?

Looking back on K'Sup Nri's story from beginning to end, I am determined to do whatever I can to make sure that women like her are not forgotten. There are hundreds of men imprisoned for their faith around the world today, and many of them have left behind wives and family. This raises some profound questions:

Who are these women?

What are they going through?

What do they face while their husbands are in prison?

Who cares for them and prays for them?

The Lord has kept K'Sup Nri's tears in his bottle. He has seen her hurt and felt her pain. And who are we to judge her desperate actions? But I want to believe that K'Sup Nri's life was not lived in vain. I want the tragic ending of her life to bring forth a new beginning in yours and in mine. I want to know that her death is serving a profound purpose—awakening Christians around the world to the ongoing tragedy of persecuted Christians and inspiring us to respond in prayer and support.

# HANH LY

"Bye, boys. Have a good day at school. I hope to be back before it gets dark."

"Mommy, I want to go with you," whimpered "Hanh Ly's" youngest son.

"Not today, sweetheart. I've only got permission for one person to see him this time."

CHAPTER 2

*Thank God, Mother is here to look after them,* Hanh thought. *How would I manage without her?*

Just before sunrise, before the heat began in earnest, Hanh Ly started her motorbike and headed north, wearing her straw hat and long elbow-length gloves to protect herself from the hot sun.

> No servant is greater than his master. If they persecuted me, they will persecute you also.
>
> *John 15:20*

## A LONG RIDE

Riding as fast as she could, Hanh barely noticed the beautiful scenery of Vietnam's central highlands. She passed emerald-green rice paddies, where workers were beginning their daily routine. In the distance, pale lavender mountains were still partly concealed by the morning mist.

Hrey tribeswomen, belonging to one of Vietnam's ethnic minority groups, walked along the road garbed in long, black tribal skirts and colorfully embroidered tops. It often amazed Hanh how those fragile-looking women could walk such long distances with heavy loads of firewood on their backs. Today she paid no attention to them.

It was all Hanh could do to concentrate on the ribbon of asphalt that stretched out before her. Part of the tarmac was covered with rice, left there to dry in the hot sun. Chickens and little children sometimes darted across the road unexpectedly. She needed to pay attention all the time, but this morning that was hard to do. The sixty-mile trip to her destination seemed endless, and her mind was with her husband.

Today was the one day of the month she was permitted to go and see him. At least that's what she hoped. A week before, she had pleaded with the local authorities in the town where she lived, and they had reluctantly granted a permit for her to visit the prison. But she knew only too well that written permission didn't guarantee anything. She had been turned away at the prison gate by unfriendly guards many times before.

Hanh longed to see Nguyen. She had talked to him only a few times since that Sunday morning in November 1994, nearly a year past, when the police abruptly entered their house. A group of Christians were gathered there to worship the Lord and study the Bible together. When the police ordered them to stop the meeting, the believers ignored them, continuing their praise and worship. The subsequent police report stated that the Christians "fought against the government's decree and fought against the officer on duty."

The police ordered everyone present to sign the report. They all refused.

That same afternoon the officers returned to Hanh and Nguyen's house. They ordered Nguyen and the other elder of the church, Brother Vinh, to go to the police station for an "inquiry." Nguyen never came home. He and Vinh had been arrested on the spot. Half a year later, on May 23, 1995, the court had sentenced them both to twenty-four months in prison for the crime of "using muscular strength to fight against an officer on duty."

Hanh knew that was not the real reason Nguyen was in prison. He had never fought with the policemen. A couple of years before he might have been guilty of far worse, but not since his life had so radically changed.

## A NEW BEGINNING

As her motorbike carried her through the fresh morning air, Hanh remembered the way their lives had been transformed during the last couple of years. In spite of everything, she had to smile. It had all started in early 1992, when two church workers from Danang had visited their town. Her husband, Nguyen, had known them from his student years at United World Mission High School.

Nguyen had been a faithful member of the Christian youth group as a teenager. But when the Communists took over South Vietnam in 1975, he had been forced to return to his hometown in the central highlands. There he had lost contact with the church. Before long he'd returned to a lifestyle common to many Vietnamese and tribal people, one which revolved around alcohol.

When Nguyen's two friends from high school arrived, they shared the good news about Jesus Christ with Nguyen and his family. As Nguyen listened, the Holy Spirit convicted him of sin. On the very first day of the evangelists' visit, he decided to ask the Lord's forgiveness and rededicated his life to Jesus Christ.

The change in Nguyen was dramatic. The first thing he did was quit drinking. From a bad-tempered, foul-mouthed man, he was transformed into a loving father and a friend who spoke words of healing. Many people followed Nguyen's example and started to follow the God of the Christians, too. Hanh was one of the first to realize that she, too, needed the forgiveness of Christ.

*Tin Lanh*—Good News—had indeed come to their village. More and more lives were changed. Miracles were reported. Sick people were healed when the Christians prayed for them. Demon-possessed men and women were delivered by the power of Christ.

But not everyone was pleased with the changes in the community. The sudden drop in alcohol and cigarette sales meant a significant loss in tax revenue for the government. Local Communist cadres began to monitor Nguyen and his friend Vinh, whose life also had turned around drastically since he'd accepted Christ.

Meanwhile Nguyen and Vinh became fervent evangelists. After witnessing to their Vietnamese friends, they also began to reach out to the Hrey people.

Ethnic minorities in Vietnam had been the subjects of severe repression and persecution since the Communist takeover. Their churches had been closed, and many of their pastors spent years in prison. After the North Vietnamese seized control of the country, Christians had been scattered and often isolated. Only a handful of

Christian tribespeople found their way to the coastal towns and asked for help from Vietnamese pastors. Meeting in homes, many of them had continued to worship the Lord in secret.

Hanh knew that when Nguyen began to share the gospel with the Hrey tribe, he would be in trouble. Having training sessions in their homes to teach new Hrey believers was strictly forbidden by the government. The authorities preferred that the tribal people remain ignorant, steeped in their old ways of animism. Educated tribal people might pose a threat to the Communist regime. In the past many of them had fought valiantly against the Communist insurgents.

When Nguyen and Vinh were arrested, it had not come as a surprise to Hanh, nor to Vinh's wife, Deng. But it had been devastating to them and their children.

## FIFTEEN PRECIOUS MINUTES

Now as she made her way across the countryside to see her husband, Hanh prayed, *O, Lord, please let them be nice to me today—please! There's so much I want to tell him.* She tried to think through everything that she wanted to say.

In just fifteen minutes she would never be able to tell him all about the children. She longed to talk to him about Duc, their oldest. Duc was doing exceptionally well in school, and he often went out of his way to help his mother. The other boys pitched in where they could, too, getting water from the well and running little errands for her. Little Uc seemed to miss his father the most. He always begged her to take him along when she prepared to visit the prison.

Hanh knew that the children suffered because the family had so little money. But although they all had their bad days, as children do, they rarely complained. The older boys helped her tend the small vegetable garden that supplemented their diet. Most important, they were all good boys, helpful boys, godly boys. It was important for Nguyen to know that. It would make him proud.

Hanh also wanted to tell Nguyen about the many people who were coming to Christ. Since his arrest, the number of house churches in their area had grown from twelve to forty-five. *I must remember to tell him that,* Hanh reminded herself. *He'll be so happy.*

But should she tell him that more pastors and leaders had been arrested? In their province alone, there were now seven Christian workers in prison. Did he really need to know that the government had taken away land from the tribal people, and that the children of Hrey Christians were no longer permitted to go to school? Maybe these things would make him sad. Maybe she should just tell him the good news.

Oh yes, and what about Minh? She had come down from North Vietnam to teach at the local Vietnamese school. Nguyen knew her well because she had become a close family friend. But when the authorities found out that she had become a Christian, they had fired her. Should she tell him that?

*No, maybe not,* Hanh concluded. These stories would only cause Nguyen to feel depressed. She should keep them to herself. It would be best to just listen to her husband. Let him ask the questions and tell her about whatever was bothering him.

There was so much she wanted to know about Nguyen's circumstances. How was he being treated? Someone told her that prisoners were often made to stand outside in the hot sun for hours on end. She must remember to ask him if it was true. And did he have opportunities to share Christ with others? If that were so, Hanh would be relieved. That would help Nguyen see God's purpose in all the hardships.

The miles flew by, and the sun's heat was now bearing down heavily on Hanh. At long last she left the countryside and entered a more populated area. The prison was nearby. The closer she came to the end of her journey, the more her anxiety grew. It was nearly lunchtime, so she decided to stop for a bowl of noodle soup at one of the many food stalls that lined the street. It would not be good to arrive at the prison right then, she reasoned. If the guards were hungry, they would be even more irritable than usual. Maybe after lunch they would feel less hostile.

Hanh absently ate her noodles, her mind still racing. Finally, after an hour had passed, she drove her motorbike to the prison gate and parked it outside.

## ORDERS FROM ABOVE

Weary from the long trip, her hands shaking with anxiety, she showed a guard the document that she'd received from the local police. It stated that on that specific date she would be granted a fifteen-minute visit with her husband.

The guard glanced disinterestedly at the paper and told her to wait in a shaded area. Trying to calm herself, Hanh took a few deep breaths and sat down on one of the benches that lined the prison wall. After about half an hour the guard returned with her paper.

"Sorry, your husband can't receive you today."

"But why not? I have permission!" Tears burned in Hanh's eyes. "Why can't he see me? Is he sick?"

The guard shrugged impassively. "He can't see you. That's all I can tell you."

"You can't just deny me entrance!" Hanh's voice grew shrill. "*Please* let me see him. I've traveled sixty miles to come here!"

Her tears and pleading were to no avail, and her desperate words seemed to fall on deaf ears.

"Sorry," the guard answered, looking bored. "Orders from above."

"Can I talk to your supervisor?"

"The superintendent doesn't see visitors."

Hanh had heard it all before. In that loveless place, no meant *no*.

So she started up her bike's motor and began the long journey home. "Lord, why do these people hate us?" she prayed aloud as she rode into the afternoon breeze, her tears streaming into her hair. "Why do they treat us like this?"

For the next hour Hanh was engulfed in sadness. Life was hard for her, especially in times like this. But it was even harder for her husband. He would have to do without the extra food she had brought him. She choked up again, thinking how much he would have loved the rice cakes and mangos. At least she was free to go home and be with the children. He would have to stay in that dark, hot place for at least another year.

"Please, Lord, be with him. Help him to persevere. Take care of him, keep him healthy," Hanh prayed as she rode along. There was so much she wanted to ask the Lord. But for now she would have to concentrate on the roadway.

The sun was scorching. The road ahead of her seemed endless. As Hanh wiped away the tears and sweat from her face, the words of Jesus suddenly drifted into her mind. "'No servant is greater than his master.' If they persecuted me, they will persecute you also" (John 15:20).

Despite the intense heat and her acute disappointment, Hahn was comforted to realize that Jesus understood how she was feeling right then. And as she continued on her journey, gradually her tears stopped and the peace of the Lord returned. *God certainly knows how to lift his children up above their circumstances,* she thought.

## A Special Meeting

In 1999 I met Hanh in Ho Chi Minh city. She had come down for a time of teaching and relaxation, and when she introduced herself, I immediately recognized her name. I could hardly believe that I was actually meeting her.

After first hearing the story of K'Sup Nri, I had determined that Vietnam's persecuted wives would never again be forgotten. With that in mind, I had shared Hanh's story on several occasions because it had touched me in a very personal way. When I had read about her husband's arrest and the difficulties she experienced in visiting him, I had tried to put myself in her shoes.

How would I feel if I were only able to speak to Johan for fifteen minutes a month? What would I tell him? What would I keep to myself?

Can you put yourself in that situation? What would you say?

Now, unexpectedly, I had the opportunity to ask Hanh what life was *really* like while her husband was in prison. "Most times," she told me, "when I made the long trip to visit Nguyen, I was sent away without seeing him."

Yet now she stood before me, smiling and happy. She had survived, even though it had been a long, hard passage.

"Did you know that Nguyen is home now?" she told me excitedly. "He and Vinh were both released after two years."

Nguyen has continued to serve the Lord in freedom. "Sometimes," Hanh says, "I wish he would be more careful."

She has to remind herself that after all Jesus has done for them, she simply can't keep Nguyen to herself. He has to preach the gospel. "There are still so many people in our area who have yet to hear the Good News," she explains.

Vinh was arrested again after only one month of freedom. He is serving another two years in prison, and his wife, Deng, is having a hard time caring for their five children. And, of course, she is once more struggling with the fifteen-minute visits.

There are many women like Hanh and Deng in Vietnam. Evangelists continue to be arrested and put behind bars. Although churches are open and people appear to be free to worship in the main cities, even there the church is restricted. There is less "openness" than meets the eye. In rural areas, especially, Christians continue to be harassed and persecuted for their faith.

Despite these circumstances, the gospel cannot be bound and people continue to find freedom in Christ. The church in Vietnam is growing because evangelists like Nguyen and Vinh are willing to obey Christ no matter what it costs them. We should remember to pray for them. But let's not forget their wives—women like Hanh and Deng. These faithful believers have to struggle for survival during their husbands' imprisonments. They long for them, pray for them, wait for them, and—whenever possible—make the best of their fifteen-minute visits. They do it all for love. They do it for the sake of the gospel. They do it for the Lord.

# ALICE YUAN

## "THIS IS FROM ME"

The slightly stooped man stood waiting for us on a Beijing street corner, a wool cap pulled over his head to protect him from the freezing cold. It wasn't hard to recognize him. We'd seen his picture, we'd heard his story, we'd prayed for him for years. Now, at last, we had been invited to his home.

CHAPTER 3

After briefly shaking our hands, he led us past colorful fruit stands, past a watchful police officer, along the Lama temple, and through a narrow winding alley that led to his "house"—not much more than a room that served as both living room and bedroom. The tiny kitchen looked like an add-on, probably built later than the original structure.

*Consider the outcome of their way of life and imitate their faith.*

*Hebrews 13:7*

Alice, his wife, greeted us with a warm handshake and a radiant smile and rushed off to make us a cup of tea. As I sat down on the small couch in their living room, I could hardly believe I was really there—it was almost too good to be true. At last I was meeting Alice and Alan Yuan face-to-face. Johan and I were actually sitting in their house!

## WORSHIP WITH CHINA'S HIDDEN BELIEVERS

People from all over the world have visited Pastor Alan Yuan and his wife, Alice, since China reopened its borders to tourists. Over the years many Bible couriers have been touched by the lives of these two dear people when visiting their home. The way Alan and Alice have been consistently faithful to their Lord has served as a powerful example to us all.

Pastor Alan, now eighty-four years old, handed a written testimony to us and the other visitors who had come to see them. Only one sentence was devoted to his wife, Alice, but it spoke volumes: "During the twenty-two years of my imprisonment, my wife suffered untold hardship in bringing up the children."

After reading these words, I looked up at Alice. Tiny and bent a little with age, Alice Yuan was still a beautiful woman; her face wreathed in smiles of welcome and warmth. She did not look like a woman who should be pitied. Like so many faithful Chinese who have suffered for their faith, her face seemed illuminated with an inner light that shone in her eyes.

I had heard about some of the hardships this courageous woman had faced, and I longed for an opportunity to sit and talk with her about her experiences. But for the moment she was far too busy for conversation. Visitors needed tea. And tangerines. And roasted chestnuts. And as if that were not enough, bananas were brought in. Despite their poverty, the Yuans were incredibly hospitable.

As I looked around the room, following Alice's busy movements, for a moment my thoughts went back to Holland. That very day, Johan's mother was celebrating her birthday, and she was now Alice's age—seventy-nine. But how different her life had been from Alice's.

Thinking of the people in the retirement home where my mother-in-law lives, I could not help but compare their lives to that of Alice Yuan. Physically it was certainly much easier to live in affluent Holland than in China. But as far as fulfilling lives went, I think Alice had the better deal. Even at her age she regularly spent nights at the police station because she and Alan continued to be harassed by the authorities. And modern comforts were totally absent from their little abode.

But Alice was thankful she and her husband were still being used by the Lord. With her many visitors, she had no time to be bored. She also had little time to concentrate on all the aches and pains that so often accompany old age. The warm smile on her face proved to me that the Lord is no one's debtor. He has his own ways of making up to us what we sacrifice for him.

"We were told that the authorities had forced you to close your house church," Johan said to Alan, "so we didn't expect to be able to visit you like this."

"Well, the people keep coming back, so I have to let them in," the old man answered with a grin.

I glanced around the room. A picture of Billy Graham was clearly visible on the wall next to a hanging, which quoted John 14:6 written in Chinese characters: "Jesus answered, 'I am the way and the truth and the life. No one comes to the Father except through me.'"

The room was sparsely furnished. A double bed, a small dining table, a wardrobe, and a small couch were backed against the wall to save space. Lots of folding chairs were placed closely together. Boxes overflowing with cassettes, and a few books were piled atop a cupboard.

All the while, an endless stream of young people flooded the Yuan's apartment. Even after I thought the room was completely packed, still more visitors continued to arrive. "Auntie Alice" kept bringing in more and more folding chairs. Several girls sat on the bed behind Johan. Their faces were so different; it almost seemed as if they'd all come from different countries. Some looked very Chinese, but others reminded us of the tribal people we had met in Vietnam. Still others had Mongolian features.

I had heard that house church meetings are packed to over-flowing, but this exceeded my wildest imagination. Once you were seated, you had to stay where you were. There was no way out until the ones closest to the door left the apartment. *It's a good thing they don't have fire regulations,* I told myself. *Half the people wouldn't be here. And if a fire breaks out, we're not going anywhere!*

But all those thoughts vanished when the worship began. Tears welled in my eyes as I recalled the countless prayer meetings I had attended over the years. One meeting stood out in particular—in 1971 at our Bible college. At that time visiting Hong Kong mission-aries could only show us pictures of distant China taken from a hill-top in the New Territories. The doors to the People's Republic were still tightly closed. All we really knew was that there were many Christians inside and that they were persecuted. So that night we had fervently prayed for our brothers and sisters.

Now, more than three decades later, I was actually worshiping with those faithful Chinese believers.

I glanced at Johan, and his face was beaming. There was no place in the whole world he would have rather been. What a privilege it was for us to meet these saints, Alan and Alice Yuan.

Alan had kept his faith in prison; he lived for almost twenty-two years without a Bible and without his family. Even now, with this large gathering in his tiny apartment, Alan did not seem to worry at all about possible repercussions. I couldn't help but think about the policeman we had past just a few yards away from the Yuan's house.

As for Alice, I knew that my conversations with her would be well worth the wait. As the evening progressed, one by one and two by two, many of the young people quietly excused themselves and headed for home. Before long, most everyone had left. The moment I had waited for had finally arrived. Alice Yuan had time to talk to me.

## LED BY THE FAITHFUL SHEPHERD

"For many years I've prayed for you," I told her. "I want so much to hear about your experiences for myself."

Alice nodded and patted my hand. "Thank you for praying," she said. As she smiled and began her story, I realized that what she had to say wasn't new to me after all.

In April 1958 Alan and several other pastors had been arrested and taken to prison. "You will never see him again!" a Communist officer coldly informed Alice as her husband was led away. Her eyes swam, and her heart ached with the sudden loss. The future looked hopeless. How could she live without the love of her life? What did she have to live for without her ministry partner?

Alan and Alice had enthusiastically served the Lord together since their marriage in 1937. First they had gone to work in the countryside of Hebei Province. The evangelistic services they'd held in different villages there had lasted for three or four days at a time. Together the Yuans had rejoiced to see dozens of people come to Christ during their tent meetings.

The Communists surrounded their area in 1945, and tensions increased. Meanwhile, a letter from Beijing informed Alan that his unsaved mother was very ill. He and his young wife hurried back to the city, as Alan was her only child. What an answer to prayer it was to see not only Alan's mother but also his grandmother come to a saving knowledge of Jesus Christ.

But by then the Communists had destroyed all the railways around the big cities, so Alan and Alice were forced to stay in Beijing. But they weren't idle. They started holding street meetings, and before long a new church was founded where twenty to fifty new Christians were baptized each year.

Then came liberation in 1949. Once the Maoist Communists took control of the country and established the "People's Republic," street meetings were no longer allowed in China. Western Christian missionaries were no longer welcome. Things got progressively worse as more and more limitations were forced upon believers.

Along with eleven other preachers of Beijing's sixty churches, Alan Yuan refused to comply with an intolerable new law that all churches should be registered under the Three Self Patriotic movement. The Three Self Patriotic movement was headed by the government's Religious Affairs Bureau (RAB), which controlled all religious activity. The pastors were unwilling to allow their churches to become instruments of the Communist government and the RAB. So one after another, Alan and his eleven fellow pastors were arrested and imprisoned.

After Alan was locked up, Alice faced an enormous ordeal of her own. She had to care for herself and seven family members—six children and her mother-in-law—without a job or an income. Because Alan was considered an antirevolutionary, no relatives, friends, or fellow Christians dared to see her. Alice was alone except for the immediate family for whom she had full responsibility.

The uncertain future and the huge obligations Alice faced seemed unbearable to her. How on earth could she carry on?

"I had a very hard time at the beginning," Alice told me, shaking her head. "I knew that my husband was in prison for the Lord, but the burden on my shoulders was just too much for me."

"I can't carry it, Lord," she prayed again and again. For several terrible days, Alice Yuan tried to wrestle with God. But the more she wept and complained, the more heaviness she felt in her heart. Her future seemed like an impenetrable dark cloud—no way through it and no way around it.

Then one day the Lord spoke to Alice. *This was from me!* he told her. His unmistakable voice resounded in her heart.

That word from the Lord burst to life in Alice's spirit. At last she was able to surrender.

"If this was from you," she prayed, "then I will be silent. But you have to keep us and protect us. And please—don't let any of our family members shame or insult your name because of our weakness."

Alice's weighty burden lightened as she prayed, but her struggle was far from over.

Alan Yuan was imprisoned for twenty-one years and eight months. And for Alice, those years were marked by long hours of heavy physical work, by agonizing loneliness, and by times of great doubt and uncertainty.

During the years of separation from her husband, Psalm 23 was a source of comfort for Alice. She entrusted her life to those beloved verses. In fact, the promises written down in Psalm 23 became her own story:

The Lord is my shepherd, I shall not be in want.
He makes me lie down in green pastures,
he leads me beside quiet waters
he restores my soul.
He guides me in paths of righteousness
for his name's sake.
Even though I walk
through the valley of the shadow of death,
I will fear no evil,
for you are with me;
your rod and your staff,
they comfort me.

You prepare a table before me
in the presence of my enemies.
You anoint my head with oil;

my cup overflows.
Surely goodness and love will follow me
all the days of my life,
and I will dwell in the house of the Lord
forever.

## A TEST OF PHYSICAL SURVIVAL

"As I look back across those times," Alice told me, "I think God gave me four tests that he wanted me to pass."

First came the test of physical survival. The Yuan's youngest child was six years old and their oldest was seventeen when Alan was arrested. Alice was the only person who could work to earn a living in the family, and she simply couldn't work hard enough to provide for all of them. One day the family completely ran out of food. Weary and discouraged, Alice got on her knees before she went to bed. "Lord, if you don't send us some food, all I'll have to feed the children tomorrow will be boiled water. And it's not enough to fill their tummies, Lord," she reminded him.

Into Alice's mind came Jesus' promise found in Matthew 6:26. Hadn't he promised to feed even the birds of the air? After that, Alice went to sleep, confident that somehow, someway, the Lord would provide.

Early the next morning as Alice was preparing herself to face another day, there was a knock at the door. Outside stood an elderly woman, someone whom Alice had never seen before.

"Are you Sister Alice?" she asked, "and is your husband Pastor Yuan?"

"Yes . . . ," Alice murmured, wondering who the woman was and what she wanted.

As soon as Alice answered affirmatively, the old lady continued, "I've been looking for you for a couple of days, but I couldn't locate you. I didn't realize that you had moved since your husband was taken away. Finally I checked with the local authorities to find out your new address. Here, this is for you! Just thank the Lord."

"But who are you?" Alice asked, a bit perplexed by the mysterious visitor.

"I can't tell you," the woman replied. "All I can say is that the Holy Spirit told me to come and see you."

With that, she turned quickly and left before Alice could stop her.

Alice eagerly opened the box that the woman had placed in her hands. Inside was a large bag of rice, some meat and vegetables, and an envelope containing 50 RMB (US $6) in cash—a huge sum of money in those days. Alice and the family praised God, profoundly reassured that God knew how to take care of them despite Alan's absence.

Six months after Pastor Yuan was put in prison, Alice found a job as an accountant in one of the government's construction units. If she worked the whole month without taking any days off, her monthly wages were 24 RMB (US $3). Her income was not nearly enough to cover her family's expenses, but the Holy Spirit continued to move Christian brothers and sisters she had never met to provide for their needs.

Again and again Alice found envelopes stuffed with money in front of her door. Whenever she received a check, she would write a thank-you note to the person whose name, street, and city was printed on the check. Every time her letter was returned marked with the notation "No such person at this address."

## FACING POLITICAL TESTS

"My second test," Alice continued, "was that of political pressure. It was, perhaps, the most difficult."

At work Alice endured endless discrimination and humiliation. Her unit and, in fact, the entire workforce knew she was from an antirevolutionary family. Her coworkers gave her the cold shoulder, treating her like the lowest of the low. She was not invited to participate in any social activities or allowed to express her opinion at workers' meetings. When other workers received various perks, honors, and awards, Alice was always lined up with them in front of everybody else only to be intentionally ignored.

The first time this happened, Alice was both hurt and humiliated. But then unexpectedly she once again heard the voice of the

Lord. *I will write down your name in the Book of Life, and I will reward you in heaven.*

Alice felt a warm sense of comfort. A heavenly reward was a wonderful promise, but most of all, she was reminded of the Lord's love for her. And that love was what she needed the most.

Unfortunately, Alice wasn't the only one to lose rights and privileges—her children suffered, too. As most mothers would agree, this was worse than almost anything else. "It was harder to bear than my own pain," she told me.

After one of her sons was old enough to work, he was hired at a local factory. That particular facility received a special reward every year for being one of the best factories in the area. But because of his father's circumstances, the Yuan's son never received any recognition. Like Alice, he was blatantly overlooked.

Another son, after graduation from high school, was denied employment in Beijing. All his classmates were assigned by the government to different work units within the city, but he never received a notice. Instead, he was sent to work in Ning Xiah province, in a remote, rural area. This, again, because his father was considered antirevolutionary.

Her boys had worked hard, diligently, and faithfully. "It's not fair!" she cried out to the Lord again and again when she saw them hurt and rejected. And again and again the Lord reminded her of the sufferings of his only begotten Son.

Alice was hard-pressed on every side. But the more pressured she was, the more grace she seemed to receive. She was forced to endure the abuse of one of China's notorious political "self-criticism" groups. For six months interrogators demanded that she renounce her faith and divorce her husband. "Surely, you realize," they mocked her again and again, "that he will never return. Don't you understand that he has received a sentence of *life imprisonment?*"

"Yes, I do understand," she quietly responded. "But I cannot and will not divorce him."

This infuriated the group, who also accused her of corruption. "We really don't understand how you can possibly feed a family of eight on the little money you make. You are obviously hiding something from us!"

The group tried to intimidate Alice into pleading guilty to their charges, but Alice stood her ground.

"And the Lord strengthened me," she told me, "with the words of Proverbs 24:10: 'If you falter in times of trouble, how small is your strength!' Besides, nobody could find any proof of the accusations against me."

As the public criticism, examinations, and trials continued over the years, Alice never saw a single smiling face. Everybody was determined to break her. Others broke—one man she knew was placed in a mental hospital because of the intolerable pressure his persecutors had exerted against him. Alice could only thank the Lord for giving her the strength to endure.

## Strength to Meet the Test

"My third test," Alice continued, "was the very heavy workload I had to carry. At first I was able to work in a construction company as an accountant. After three days on the job, the leader trusted me so much that he put me in charge of all the bookkeeping and accounting. The Lord gave me the wisdom and strength to do that work for eight years."

Then the Cultural Revolution began in 1966. The street corners were full of young revolutionaries, scanning lists that named people belonging to antirevolutionary families. These zealous young Communists took it upon themselves to demand that anyone remotely questionable be removed from their positions of employment and forced to work in the fields.

It was a time of great terror and bloodshed. Families were torn apart, and fear ruled the country without a hint of mercy. Alice was not immune to the terrible apprehension that gripped everyone during those days of anarchy, and she was not surprised when her supervisor came and told her she would have to transfer to a brick factory to do heavy manual labor.

Alice Yuan had never done hard labor in her life, and in her physical weakness, she had to rely on the Lord's strength. The first day on the job, she was ordered to load and unload 150 bricks off a handcart, which she was supposed to push to and from various places in the factory. She only had fifteen minutes per trip, and everyday she had to meet her quota. Feeling desperate and afraid, she could only pray. And somehow she got through each day.

During January and February, the coldest months of the year, Alice and her coworkers were sent to build a swimming pool beside a frozen river. They had to move heavy and unwieldy construction materials with their handcarts across the icebound waterway. The wind was piercingly cold, and the pain in Alice's hands and feet was even more excruciating than the exhaustion in her limbs. She could barely move.

Some unbelievers dropped their handcarts, sat down on the frozen river, and wept. Most of the workers could not meet their quota. But tiny Alice Yuan received so much strength from the Lord that she was able not only to complete her goal but to even exceed her quota. Many of her associates and leaders were astonished. "Where does she get her energy?" they asked each other.

Only Alice knew.

## Marriage Vows Put to the Test

The last test Alice had to pass was the temptation to remarry. Like K'Sup Nri, Alice also struggled with overwhelming loneliness. She cruelly missed the warm embrace and the encouraging words of her beloved husband. She had been in her thirties when Alan was taken away. And she was almost afraid to dream of his return for fear that day would never come.

And that's where temptation came into the picture. Seeing her endless emotional desolation, people tried to introduce her to prospective boyfriends.

Not only was Alice inconsolably lonely, but she was severely disadvantaged by her family's antirevolutionary stigma. She knew very well that the only way to remove that stigma would be to divorce Alan and to marry someone else. One genuinely nice man offered his love and support to her, and it was a struggle—both spiritually and emotionally—not to be swept away by his gracious attention. Pretty and charming as she was, Alice was offered clothes, money, and all kinds of gifts on other occasions from interested suitors.

One gentleman actually prepared divorce documents, pointing out that all she had to do was sign them. "Once you're free of him," he explained with a kind smile, "you will be able to move into a better apartment. You'll have a good life, and your children will have no more worries about food."

Seeing her so happily reunited with her husband, these stories may not seem especially significant. But for Alice, at the time the temptation was intense. Nearly everyone told her that Alan would never return, and at times she was inclined to believe them. Yet somehow—in spite of the relief a divorce would provide—she refused to sign the papers.

"I overcame the temptation by trusting the Lord," she told me, the sad expression on her face briefly mirroring the pain she had suffered. "When I got married, I made a vow and covenant before the Lord that in health, sickness, rejoicing, and mourning I would follow my husband until we saw our Lord."

And so, one after the other, Alice Yuan simply told the men who tried to court her that she was married to Alan, and she would remain married to him until the day of his release—or until she knew for sure that he had died.

## A PRAYER FOR THE FUTURE

But Alan Yuan did not die. After twenty-one years and eight months he returned home to his loving wife. For both of them the reunion was nothing short of a miracle. "By the time he was reunited with us, the children were all grown up with families of their own," she said with a smile. "So I had him all to myself."

Alice proudly showed me her most recent family picture, which was taken at their sixtieth wedding anniversary. Six children and ten grandchildren surround the beaming elderly couple.

"Alice, do they all follow the Lord?" I asked.

"Some more than others," she answered with a shrug of her shoulders and a sad smile.

*No different from our families in the free world*, I thought.

By now everyone had left the meeting. The hour was growing

late, and it was time for us to go, too. However, Johan and I had one final question: "How can we pray for you?"

The Yuan's answer should not have surprised us. It was not a request for physical health or material goods. It was not an appeal for safety and protection from the authorities, even though Alan and Alice continued to face strong opposition from the Chinese government. No, after a life of service to their Lord, Alice and Alan asked that we pray for the most important burden on their hearts.

"Please pray that more people in our country will come to Christ," Alan Yuan said. "It's very important, you know, because Jesus is coming soon!"

# MARY WU

"The harvest is plentiful. . . . The harvest is plentiful. . . ."

Almost like a chant the words repeated over and over in "Mary Wu's" mind as she labored in the field. Sweat streamed

CHAPTER

The harvest is plentiful but the workers are few. Ask the Lord of the harvest, therefore, to send out workers into his harvest field.

*Matthew 9:37-38*

down her angular face, and she had to wipe it away to glance at the clear sky—not one cloud offered a moment's respite from the relentless sun. She straightened herself up and rested on the hoe, her back stiff and sore. Mary had worked in the overpowering heat all day, and she felt almost unable to walk.

"Mommy, I'm so hungry!" moaned five-year-old Wang, absently pulling out a weed.

"Yes, darling, I am too. It's almost time to go home."

The harvest indeed was plentiful that year. The wheat was almost ready to be reaped, and the corn, too, was thriving.

Yes, the Lord had blessed them. Mary had reason to be thankful, yet her body ached from head to toe, and she had no energy. To make matters worse, her heart was heavy.

There was still so much work to do, and as usual she had to do it alone. She was never able to get used to the hard physical labor, and as she watched her neighbors in their fields, she couldn't help but feel a twinge of jealousy. Husbands and wives worked together, hoeing their way through the almost-ripe crops. How long had it been since her husband had been there with her?

"The harvest is plentiful, but the workers are few. . . ."

As she picked up her little boy to carry him back to the house, the words of Jesus again echoed in her mind. All at once she recog-

34

nized the link to her situation. Of course! The spiritual harvest in China was plentiful, too. Millions of people were still awaiting the gospel message. And her husband, Sung, was one of the workers who had gone out into God's fields. She might be slaving away out there in the hot sun, but in spiritual terms so was he. And Mary knew that her husband was indeed one of God's special workers in China.

How did I hear about Mary Wu? I've had the exciting opportunity to visit China a few times and to carry a few Bibles along with me to pass on to others. As I've met up with the believers and heard stories about what life is like for the courageous men who distribute God's Word throughout the countryside, I've also learned about their brave and faithful wives who keep their families together during lengthy absences, through times of uncertainty, and even during their husbands' imprisonments. Sung and Mary are just such a couple.

## GOD'S SPECIAL WORKERS

One day an itinerant preacher visited their small village, located in one of China's central provinces. At the end of the evangelistic service, Sung accepted Jesus Christ into his life. At first Mary was skeptical, but not for long. What a difference that decision made in her husband! All at once his life took on new meaning. Apart from receiving forgiveness for everything he had ever done wrong, Sung gained hope for the future and a purpose for living.

It wasn't long before Mary, too, came to Christ, and she was just as excited about her faith as her husband. In their enthusiasm, the two of them often talked late into the night, wondering what they could do to spread the good news about Jesus. They wanted the world to know about the miraculous new life that they were experiencing.

One night, just as they were about to fall asleep, Sung said, "Wherever Jesus leads, I'll follow."

"I'll follow too," Mary solemnly agreed.

Could they have imagined what that promise would mean?

It wasn't long before Sung was invited to accompany a pastor on an evangelistic trip to an area where the gospel had not yet been preached. Sung was thrilled with the opportunity, which he saw as an answer to prayer. But his parents, who shared the house with him and Mary, weren't the least bit impressed with his plans. It wasn't that they were really opposed to Sung's Christian beliefs; they just didn't like the consequences.

"Son, you are needed at home," Sung's father pleaded. "There's so much work to be done in the fields." The older man pointed out that the extra money Sung made by occasionally working in a nearby factory was also a huge help. Because his parents were getting along in years, they had become dependent on Sung and Mary's care.

Mary, who had prayed with her husband for guidance, didn't object to his going. She assumed that he would only be gone a few days, and she was happy that her husband would be sharing the Good News with others. Perhaps if she had known what was coming, Mary might have approached Sung's journey with more reluctance.

Instead of days, Sung and the pastor were gone for weeks. When they finally came home, they were exhausted. But as Sung told Mary about the people he had met, his face glowed with joy. "So many people came to Christ, Mary! And they wouldn't have known about him if we hadn't told them. They pleaded with us to come back soon to teach them more about Jesus!"

As they got ready for bed, she turned toward him. "So you're leaving again?" Mary asked softly.

Sung didn't seem to hear her. "But, oh, how I wish we had brought more Bibles to give them," he sighed as they finally lay down to sleep. "If they could read God's Word for themselves, they would be able to grow in their faith. I'm just so sorry we had only a few copies of God's Word with us. Pastor told me that we may be able to get some more in Guangzhou. Brother Li lives there, you know, and he has contacts. Sometimes people from abroad bring him Scriptures. Maybe we can get some from him."

Mary could hardly believe her ears. "So you're leaving me again?" she asked again, this time a little more forcefully. "Sung, you've been gone for weeks, and you've just come home!" Mary paused, fighting back her tears. "Sung, please listen to me. The wheat field needs to be hoed, and I can't do it all by myself!"

"Okay, okay . . ." Sung nodded, by now barely able to keep his eyes open. "I understand. But let's talk about this some more tomorrow. We need to get some sleep first."

Sung managed to stay home for a few days, and he did what he could to help Mary in the field. But his mind was clearly elsewhere. Finally one day he sat down with Mary, took her hands in his, and said, "Please understand, Mary. I love you with all my heart. But I need to go and get more Bibles."

Mary fought away her tears and nodded her head silently. Fears nagged at her, resentment swelled inside her, but what could she do? She wished Sung well and tried to smooth things over with his parents. Meanwhile, their pastor was only too happy to write a letter of recommendation for Sung so the Bible distributor he was going to see would know he could be trusted.

Giving Bibles to strangers is dangerous business in China. Yes, it is possible to buy Bibles in Nanjing from the officially approved printing press, but the publishers there do not produce nearly enough to provide for the countless and fast-growing house churches in the countryside.

Furthermore, if you want to buy a Bible from the official press, you are required to register your name to receive it, and Christians in the house churches don't especially like to do that. They prefer to operate without dealing with the government at all. And this carries its own risks. Chinese law states that there is free- dom in China *not* to believe. Giving a Chinese citizen a Bible is interpreted by the authorities as intruding on his or her freedom not to believe. In short, distributing Bibles in China can lead to arrest and imprisonment.

Had Sung and Mary counted the cost? When they first met the Lord, they had agreed that they would obey him no matter what he asked them to do. But now he was leading Sung to do something very costly, indeed, and leaving Mary with a huge burden of work in the process. Of course Sung's mission was important. That's why Mary was willing to wait for him at home. She felt lonely, exhausted, and afraid, but she knew Sung was doing this for Jesus, which helped her cope.

## UNWELCOME VISITORS

After Sung's second departure, and after more than a week of waiting, Mary spotted a small figure coming toward her on the road that led to their town. The walk was unmistakably familiar.

"Wang, Daddy's coming!" she shouted to her little son who was playing at the back of the house. "Let's go help him carry his bags."

Together they ran to greet him.

"Sung, these bags are incredibly heavy!" Mary groaned, trying to lift one onto her back.

Sung laughed. "They are heavy! The only thing that makes them feel a little lighter is knowing that God's Word is inside them."

For the past few days, during his long journey home, Sung had carried the Bibles on and off trains and buses. "At least the police didn't inspect my luggage," he pointed out, "and that was a direct answer to prayer. There was no X-ray machine in use at any of the train stations."

"This must be a good time of the year to transport Bibles," said Mary, smiling.

The couple and their little boy happily returned to their house and hid the Bibles beneath the wooden floor. But now that Sung had the Bibles, he wanted to take them to the new believers as soon as possible.

Sung planned his next trip, and as he and Mary talked they gradually began to realize that their lives had changed forever. Already, Sung was gone more than he was at home. Before long, he would always be on the road, always trying to share the gospel with those who were hungry for the truth, and always searching for Bibles and training literature for the new believers.

As months passed into years, Mary found it harder to contend with Sung's absences. His parents were getting older, and they were no longer able to help her as much as they had in the past. Wang was growing up, and it really was a challenge for her to raise him alone, with his father gone so much.

During this time the number of Christians in their town continually increased, and so did Mary's responsibilities in the church. Other women would come to her house to seek her counsel. And

Mary did not complain, in fact, complaining never crossed her mind. Chinese Christians are taught from the start that they will always have to put God before anything else. For them, family and personal needs must take second place. But Mary was overwhelmed with responsibility. And to make matters worse—godly as she was—she never seemed to stop worrying.

As Sung became more and more involved in the work of Bible distribution, Mary realized that he was in constant danger. Occasionally she heard of Christian men being arrested and sentenced to pay large fines or even go to prison for distributing unauthorized Bibles.

She often lay awake at night, wondering about her husband. *Where is he?* she'd silently ask herself. *What's he doing? When will he come home?* During the day her eyes perpetually scanned the road, searching for Sung's familiar stride. Every time she saw a distant figure coming her way, she thought, *Is it Sung? Is he back?*

The uncertainty was sometimes almost too much to bear. God comforted Mary when she read his Word, and she could tell him about her fears and her loneliness.

"But, Lord," she prayed one night, "couldn't you just send me someone I can talk to? Someone I can really open up with and share my heart? I need someone I can trust. Someone who will listen to me. And please—find someone who won't condemn me for worrying and for feeling sorry for myself now and then."

One day when Mary had just started to cook dinner, she was startled by a sudden knock on the door.

"Open up! Police!" a strident voice commanded.

Her heart pounding and her hands trembling, she pulled the door open. Outside stood two policemen dressed in the green uniforms of the Public Security Bureau.

"Where is your husband?" they demanded, marching into the house.

"I don't know," Mary answered truthfully. "He's traveling, and I don't know when he is coming back."

"And where are the Bibles?" the uninvited visitors barked. They continued their questioning while pulling the mattress off Mary's bed, dumping out drawers, and searching through cupboards.

"I only have one Bible—my own," Mary answered, keeping her voice as calm as she could. Trying to control her shaky hands, she showed them her personal copy of God's Word.

"Look, we know you have more Bibles in your house. You'll save yourself a lot of trouble if you'll show us where they are."

"I can't show you anything because there are no more Bibles here!" Mary insisted. She silently thanked God that she and Sung had distributed every extra copy they had. Bibles never stayed in her house long—too many people longed to have one.

Just then Sung's parents, frightened by the noise, came to her rescue. "Leave her alone! She's here all by herself, and she is telling you the truth. There's only one Bible in this house, and you're looking at it!"

At last, angry and frustrated, the policemen stormed out, leaving behind a ransacked house. "Tell your husband to report to our office when he gets back," one of the officers shouted over his shoulder as he slammed the door behind him.

So now Mary's worst fears had been realized—the Public Security Bureau had apparently become aware of Sung's involvement in Bible distribution. "Thank you, Lord, that he wasn't home," she sighed. She was also deeply grateful that their Wang had been playing at a friend's house. She whispered a quick prayer that he hadn't seen the policemen.

## DELIVERANCE AND DISBELIEF

Mary's relief was short lived. Not many days after the incident, she received news that Sung had been arrested. "He either has to pay a 500 yuan fine or stay in prison," a Christian friend told her. "He's been accused of possessing unauthorized religious literature."

Once Mary heard the news, her mind was whirling with questions. Where in the world would she find 500 yuan? Their family earned less than 100 a month. What could she possibly do?

She decided to confide in the pastor with whom Sung had made his first mission trip. Maybe he could help her figure out what to do. She walked to his home and poured out the story to him.

He nodded, smiled, and said to her, "Of course we'll help you, Mary! Sung is serving the Lord and helping others, and now we need to help him. We'll do what we can to get him out of prison. I'll call on as many Christians as I can to help him pay his fine. You just go home and pray for him."

Mary was almost limp with relief, realizing that others really were willing to help. For the first time she began to believe that she wasn't utterly alone in this ordeal.

A few days later the man who had told her about Sung's arrest ran up to Mary's house and pounded on the door. "Mary! Are you there?" he shouted. "I've got great news!"

Mary opened the door, glancing around to see if anyone was watching.

"Mary, Sung has been released! The Lord has delivered him! He is in Shanghai, in Brother Si's house. Don't tell anybody where you're going, but please come with me. Sung really wants to see you!"

She could hardly believe her ears. "Are you sure? We haven't paid any money. How can Sung be free? How could that happen?"

Mary hurriedly asked her in-laws to take care of Wang for a few days, and as quickly as possible, on foot and then by bus, she found her way to where Sung was hiding. When she finally arrived at Brother Si's house, Sung greeted her with open arms. "Mary, I am so glad to see you. It has been so long, and I have so much to tell you!"

Quite overwhelmed by Sung's warm welcome, Mary sat down to listen. "I realize I haven't been home for a long time," he apologized, "but that is because I went all the way to Henan Province. The need for Bibles is so great there. I met one leader of a house church network who told me that he has a few hundred coworkers and about ten thousand believers in his group. Can you imagine ten thousand believers in one group?"

"Sung, that's wonderful, but—"

Sung went on as if Mary hadn't said a word. "They desperately need Bibles for the young believers and study Bibles for the leaders. They're planning to have a training session for all the coworkers. I hope we can bring them study Bibles before they meet. I know

Brother Yi is expecting a new shipment soon, and I've got to go ask him for study Bibles to take to them."

"No!" Mary interrupted, more loudly than she'd intended. "Sung, listen to me. You can't go anywhere for a while. It is just too dangerous for you right now. It seems to me that it is nothing short of a miracle you were released so quickly. You'd better keep a low profile for a while. Do you want to be arrested again?"

Mary began to cry, and she impatiently wiped the tears from her face. "Don't you understand? I've missed you, Sung. I've missed you so much. I just want you to stay home for a while. I'm so tired. Your parents are getting old. Wang needs you. The roof needs fixing. And it will be New Year's soon. Please come home for the holidays, Sung. Enough is enough."

So Sung returned home. He settled down to his domestic responsibilities without complaining, but their time together wasn't as happy as Mary had hoped. Naturally Mary and Sung's parents were thrilled to have him home. And Wang was delighted to have his father around, chattering to him constantly and showing off all the things he'd learned since Sung had left. But they soon noticed that no one was coming to visit. The other Christians in the village seemed to be avoiding the family.

It wasn't long before Mary found out why.

"Released after three days without paying any fine? He must have talked," one woman scoffed when Mary invited her and her husband to their home for a visit. "He obviously informed against other Christians. Why else would they let him go? He can't be trusted. And for that matter, neither can you!"

Sung and Mary's house had once welcomed an endless stream of guests whenever Sung came home. Now no one but their pastor came to see them. His visits were the only remnants of friendship they had left, and his prayers for them literally carried them through. It was a great comfort knowing that their pastor had never lost faith in his old traveling companion, but the mistrust of their friends cut to their very souls.

Eventually the time came for Sung to say good-bye again.

"Please be careful!" was all Mary could think of to say as she watched her husband walk away. This farewell hurt her more than all the others put together. Sung was leaving without the blessing of his friends, without the promise of their prayers, and without their farewell embraces. And once again Mary was left to deal with all the problems, all the misunderstandings, all the work.

And she was more alone than ever. *So much for all the "help" the pastor promised*, Mary thought bitterly. *They don't trust Sung. And that means they aren't going to trust me, either.*

In one sense she was relieved that Sung was gone. Ever since he had returned home, she'd lived with the constant fear that the Public Security Bureau would show up, night or day, to arrest him. She knew her husband was called—called to do God's work, called to go out into the harvest field. She was proud of him, and she supported him. But at the same time, life was difficult both with and without him.

## "Whom Should We Fear?"

In Sung's absence the Christians in town gradually started to reach out to Mary again. No one had been arrested after Sung's release, so townspeople determined that he probably hadn't betrayed anybody. Mary was relieved, and little by little she began to see that she could count on the support of the brothers and sisters again. She needed it.

Meanwhile, Sung went about his business. He was able to secure the much-needed study Bibles. "As many as you can spare, please," was his stock answer whenever he was asked how many Bibles he wanted to take.

By now, the distributors knew him well. And, yes, Sung could be trusted. No longer did they need to contact his pastor before they gave him materials. With the help of some other Christian men, he began to fill his bags with the study Bibles. It would be a heavy load to carry. And the province of Henan was far away.

But Sung had his own way of dealing with the task at hand. He simply pictured the happy faces that would greet him. Before he left on his long journey, his fellow distributors prayed for him. "Lord, please protect your precious Word and help Sung bring these Bibles to the people who long to have them. You know how they've asked you to supply their need. Use our brother and his precious cargo to answer these prayers."

The journey was long and tiresome. Sung traveled by train, by bus, and by foot. At last he arrived at his destination.

In Henan the training session was just underway when Sung showed up at the secret meeting place. He was nearly engulfed by the crowd that warmly greeted him. He quickly unloaded his precious cargo, and the pastor counted how many study Bibles he had brought.

"How did you know there were seventy coworkers studying here?" the pastor asked in surprise.

"I didn't," Sung answered.

"Well, you brought exactly seventy copies, and we have exactly seventy students! Praise the Lord!" Together they knelt down and thanked God.

Sung's visit was a great encouragement to all the young new workers who were readying themselves to go out into the Lord's harvest field. Now they could study the truth for themselves and then pass it on to others. But Sung couldn't stay long—it was much too dangerous.

Word of mouth travels fast in China. It is a much used and trusted way of passing on information, even though sometimes words get twisted around and gossip also travels fast. A few months after she'd last said good-bye to Sung, Mary heard some bad news "through the grapevine," and it seemed to be true. Sung had been arrested again. And this time his freedom could not be bought by paying a fine. He was sentenced to three years in a labor camp.

Mary's heart sank, and she wept as she told Wang and Sung's parents what had happened. But she had been mentally preparing herself for years for that very situation. Now she simply went to God, told her friends, and committed herself to pray for her husband.

Occasionally, Sung would send her a letter, and she would reply. They knew their letters were censored, so they always had to be very careful about what they wrote to each other.

After six months Mary was finally allowed to go and see her husband. All the way there she braced herself and tried to pray through her worst fears. She wasn't sure what to expect—there were numerous horror stories about sick and emaciated prisoners—unrecognizable to their wives. But to her relief Mary did not encounter a despairing, despondent husband. Instead, Sung met her with a smile on his face.

"How are you, Sung?" Mary asked. Her voice trembling with emotion, she tried to say everything at once, and the words tumbled out on top of each other. "Are you getting enough to eat? Here, I brought you some *man-tou.*" She knew how much her husband liked the special Chinese bread. "And here are some biscuits, too. How hard is the work you have to do?"

"Well, working in a stone quarry all day is exhausting, but somehow God is giving me strength to reach my quota. Oh, Mary, I wish I could explain to you how I experience God's care for me. I pray every day that he will take care of you and Wang as well. How are you managing? Tell me about the meetings. Is the fellowship growing?"

Despite their pleasure in being together, the conversation was somewhat stiff and rather frustrating. The bars between them made it impossible to touch one another. And there was no place for either of them to sit down. Still, as they stood and talked, they forgot all about the time. Soon a guard who was standing nearby glanced at his watch one last time.

"Time's up. Say good-bye," he interrupted.

Much too soon, Mary watched as her husband was led away from her. Would she ever see him again? She shook her head sadly and offered up a silent prayer of thanks that he was doing as well as he was.

On her way to the bus station, Mary quietly hummed a song that had become very dear to her since Sung's imprisonment.

"The Lord is our hiding place," she sang as she increased her pace.

> The Lord is our hiding place.
> The Lord is our strong rock.
> He went through hardship, and he is our commander,
>     he is our commander.
> With you, whom should we fear?
> You are our fortress.
> With you, whom should we fear?
> You are our fortress.

## A Special Answer to Prayer

Thinking back on her conversation with Sung, Mary reflected on how often she, too, had been amazed at the way the Lord seemed to know just what she needed. Christian friends sometimes came to bring her food at the very moment when her supplies were running low. Some of them had offered to help her gather in the harvest, which had been an immense help. Several people had volunteered to take care of Wang and Sung's parents so she could make the long trip to visit her husband.

And then one day she had a special surprise—an answer to a long-forgotten prayer. Kim, a Christian Chinese woman who was living abroad, came to visit Mary. The two had never met, but Kim had heard about Sung's detention, and she had come to tell Mary that people across the sea were praying for her.

Kim brought gifts for the family. But the greatest gift she had to offer was her willingness to listen—and listen she did. As Kim held Mary's hands, Mary poured out her heart. She told of her loneliness. She told of her fears. She told of her feelings of isolation during holidays and festivals when Sung had not been able to come home. She told about her anxiety over the years, never knowing what was happening to Sung. She told Kim how hard it had been to cope with the continuous uncertainty.

Mary's voice broke as she explained to Kim that she no longer searched the road with her eyes now that Sung was in a labor camp. She no longer hoped against hope that she would see him walking toward her. At last it was clear that he would not be coming home for a very long time. Strange as it was, in some ways that had made life easier. "I don't lie awake anymore, longing for the sound of his voice."

As Mary talked a huge burden was lifted from her heart. Through Kim's visit, God was telling her that she was important to him. He had sent one of his servants to come and listen to her because he had heard her prayers.

Mary began to cry when Kim asked her about the fellowship of believers in her town. "Kim, it is so wonderful to see God at work! It's like he's giving special grace to the house churches in China. The number of Christians continues to increase. It seems like the greater the persecution, the greater the revival. But with so many new Christians, there is such a need for Bibles. Many new believers still don't have one."

Mary paused for a moment, an idea brightening her face. "Kim, do you ever meet the people who send us the Bibles from abroad? Please thank them on our behalf and ask them to keep sending them. We need so many more. When Sung's sentence is finally over, he's going to be busy. There's a lot of work waiting for him."

Kim laughed, "But Mary, I thought you wanted nothing more than to have Sung home with you once and for all."

Mary smiled quietly and took a deep breath. "Look, I know my husband, Kim. And I know he probably won't stay home long. But I still long for his release. I guess the main reason is because it makes me happy to see him so happy serving the Lord. The harvest is plentiful. And the workers, as you know, Kim, are very few."

# SHIAO HUA

## TOO MANY GOOD-BYES

Mai, the pastor's wife, jumped off her bicycle. She dropped it outside the gate, rushed breathlessly to "Shiao Hua's" front door, and began to knock.

CHAPTER 5

Wives, submit to your husbands as to the Lord. . . . Husbands, love your wives, just as Christ loved the church and gave himself up for her.

*Ephesians 5:22, 25*

"Shiao Hua, are you there? Shiao Hua?"

The latch turned, and a slim woman stood framed in the doorway, her expression impassive. "Oh, it's you Mai," she said. "What's going on?"

Mai's round face glowed with happiness. "I'm just so happy about the news. Praise the Lord!"

"What news? What are you talking about?"

"Your husband, of course. We're so glad to hear that he's out of jail! How is he?"

"What do you mean he's out of jail?" Shiao Hua couldn't believe her ears; a frown creased her forehead. "He's still in prison, otherwise I would have known."

Mai could hardly contain her enthusiasm. "No, Shiao Hua, it's true! He's free. My husband met him at a training seminar in Brother Wang's house."

"Well, good for him then; I hope he enjoyed the meeting." Humiliation flooded through Shiao Hua and flushed her face. "It might have been nice if he'd come home first to see his family. Anyway, come on in. I'll make some tea."

She put the kettle on while Mai chattered away. But Shiao Hua wasn't listening to anything but her own dark thoughts. *That's it. I've had enough! I'm divorcing him.*

# "IT'S TOO LATE NOW!"

All day she wrestled with fears and suspicions. She wasn't clear about all the details, but one thing seemed obvious. If Tao Li cared about her at all, he would have told her himself about his release. That night as she went to bed anger toward her husband burned with increasing intensity. All the frustrations of the past, all the doubts, and all the resentments caught fire in her heart.

How could he do such a thing? For three long years she had taken care of everything. She had worked the land in his absence. She had raised their daughter all by herself. She had taken care of his mother. She had kept their house in order. She had led the church services. When her husband had been called upon by the local government to do his share of community service, she had even filled in for him, doing the heavy, manual work herself.

There had been innumerable nights with little or no sleep. Alone and afraid, she had lain awake praying for Tao Li. "Lord, please help him to stand firm. Please give him strength to fulfill his quota of hard labor. Please help him not to deny you or tell on others. And, Lord, please bring him home to us soon!"

But after all that, Tao Li was free, and she was the last to know. She had always believed that they'd loved each other wholeheartedly. Now, however, all the pieces of the puzzle were fitting together, and the picture was not a pretty one. No, this was not love.

Shiao Hua's imagination raced along like wildfire, searching for evidence and explanations. Had he met somebody else while he was in prison? Was he afraid to come and see her? Certainly he was oblivious to her needs and her feelings. Or—worse yet—he didn't care about them. Questions . . . questions . . . so many questions and no answers to be found. Nonetheless, that night Shiao Hua made her decision. She would divorce Tao Li. It was time for her to start a new life.

In the early hours of the morning she finally drifted off into an uneasy sleep. Then, just after daybreak she heard a familiar voice calling from the front door, "Shaio Hua! Shiao Hua! I'm home! I'm finally home!"

Instead of running to her husband with open arms, Shaio Hua wrapped herself in a blanket and glared at him from across the room. "Oh, so you decided to come home after all," she said. "And I'm sure you're expecting a warm welcome. Well, I'm sorry, but it's too late for that now."

Tao Li was dumbstruck. He stared at her in shock, and the tension between them was palpable as they walked into the small, tidy kitchen. He glanced around at the familiar surroundings, acutely aware of the months he'd longed to walk into his house and into his beloved wife's embrace. In his worst fears he'd never dreamed that his homecoming would be like this.

The rest of the household was still asleep, so there was no reason why Shiao Hua shouldn't say what was on her mind. "Tao Li, I've had it with you," Shiao Hua announced coldly, pouring two cups of tea.

"Even before the arrest you were gone for months at a time. For years I've put up with loneliness, endless work, and virtually no contact with you. I could take it as long as I knew we were serving the Lord together. For years I thought you hated to leave me and you went because you wanted to obey the Lord. Now I know better. I am just like any other coworker to you. You don't love me. You don't care about me. So I don't care about you anymore, either. I want a divorce!"

There was a long silence between them. Tears filled Tao Li's eyes. He was quiet for a while. "I don't understand what you're saying," he finally responded. "What have I done to make you feel this way?"

"Figure it out!" Shiao Hua snapped. "Did you come running home as soon as you were released? No! And who was the first to know her husband was a free man? Not me!"

"But Shiao Hua," he exclaimed, "I couldn't come straight here from prison. It wasn't safe to do so—it would have endangered all of you. Didn't Pastor Lei come and tell you? I asked him to!"

Quietly, his voice heavy with sadness, Tao Li began to explain his circumstances to his wife. And little by little her heart began to soften. But it would take more than a few explanations for Tao Li to convince her that he really cared for her. All her doubts and suspicions about her husband had finally come to the surface, and they weren't going to go away. In the last twenty-four hours, Shiao Hua had come to believe it was impossible for the two of them to have a happy marriage. In fact, she had seen so many struggling couples that she had almost given up on marriage itself. As far as she was concerned, marriage was a bad idea.

## COUPLES IN NEED OF GODLY COUNSEL

I have learned from our Chinese colleagues that many Chinese Christian marriages are under pressure. Many Chinese couples lack basic understanding about what it means to be a family. In rural areas, especially, the marital culture is one in which only complaints are verbalized. If a couple is doing well, nobody says anything; gratitude and encouragement are rarely expressed. Many couples know more than enough about yelling and complaining, but they haven't learned to say the words "I love you."

Meanwhile, being involved in Christian ministry always seems to intensify domestic problems. With millions of people still unaware of the gospel, with millions more pleading for Bibles, Chinese pastors believe that they cannot possibly enjoy the luxury of sitting at home and caring for their families. The Bible speaks clearly about taking up the cross and following Jesus. In fact, isn't there a verse that says that if you love your family members more than Jesus, you aren't worthy of the kingdom of Christ?

During the last decade in China the burden weighing upon spiritual leaders' wives has multiplied. Before that time, pastors were simply unable to go out and teach others. Today, opportunities for ministry abound. There are more Bibles available for distribution, and travel has become far easier. Consequently, some pastors are away from home eight to ten months out of the year. And even when they return home, relentless ministry needs crowd into their schedule.

To make matters worse, persecution by the government is still a factor to be reckoned with, especially in rural China. The government is out to control the church. Leaders of house churches who refuse to register their meetings with the government are in danger of being arrested at any time. Pastors who are imprisoned or are on the run from the police simply can't sit down, relax, and spend quality time with their families.

And, of course, spiritual pressure is fierce. As he does everywhere else in the world, Satan tries to disrupt the families of Christian leaders in China. He knows very well that the added burden will prevent them from having a fruitful ministry.

For these reasons and more, Chinese families in the ministry are paying the price. With so many demands surrounding them, husbands tend to think that it is more spiritual to do the Lord's work than to care for their families. The right balance between Christian service and family responsibility is rarely found. As a result, many wives like Shiao Hua are on the verge of an emotional breakdown, and their marriages are close to breaking up.

In the case of Tao Li and Shiao Hua the devil almost succeeded—but not quite. One day during their worst troubles, they received an invitation to attend a seminar. Aware of the challenges these couples faced, Open Doors began to conduct couples' retreats, where selected leaders and their wives specifically addressed marital concerns and difficulties. A Chinese couple from abroad came to teach biblical principles about family life.

Shiao Hua and her husband received the seminar invitation with mixed feelings. They were uncomfortable with the idea of allowing others into their personal struggles. They were scared because they were afraid their marriage was beyond repair. But they felt a great sense of excitement because they wondered if maybe— just maybe—God could show them a better way to live.

And so it was that Shiao Hua and Tao Li sat down with several other couples in a Chinese house church. They glanced around, noticing gospel posters over the door and on the walls. Above the rough, wooden pulpit, the word *Emmanuel* shone forth in Chinese characters. On another wall a world map was displayed. Otherwise the church was empty of decoration and furniture apart from rows of crude wooden benches.

When the Chinese couple from the West stood up to lead the meeting, it was immediately obvious to the group that these two people dearly loved each other. They interacted easily, seeming even to finish one another's sentences.

"This is the first time I think I've ever seen a really harmonious couple," Shiao Hua whispered to her husband, her eyes shining with hope. "Maybe marriage can work!"

Tao Li sighed and nodded. "I hope so," he whispered back.

Shiao Hua and Tao Li struggled along with the other couples to express their intimate feelings and hurts. Never in their lives had they spoken about personal matters in the presence of others, and they found it very difficult.

"I know I really need to talk to somebody," Shiao Hua said at one point, "but I'm not sure I'm ready to do it." For awhile neither she nor her husband said another word. The clock was ticking, and it was almost time for them to leave.

## OPENING THE FLOODGATES OF PAIN

Just then another teacher arrived with his wife, and Shiao Hua and Tao Li could see that there was love and harmony in their relationship, too. Somehow their faith in God and their belief that he could make their marriage work was strengthened even more.

"I think I can talk to you," Shiao Hua said shyly to the new teacher's wife.

"That's exactly what you need to do," the woman said. "And you can trust us. Believe me, we've been through plenty of troubles of our own." Her husband nodded in agreement.

So at last Shiao Hua and Tao Li opened up. Their wounds, confusion, and bitterness poured out in a torrent of words. Tears flooded both their faces.

The teaching couple listened carefully and took great care to explain the biblical principles for marriage. They provided good, practical advice about how to build a strong marital relationship. Never before in their lives had Shiao Hua and Tao Li heard such teaching.

New hope seemed to radiate from Shiao Hua's eyes. "This seminar is already making a huge difference," she confided in the teacher. "Tao Li is changing before my eyes. I know he's ready and willing to put into practice what he's learning. And there's so much to learn. By God's grace, our marriage is going to make it."

And that was not the end of the story. When Tao Li returned home, he called a special gathering of coworkers together. He invited all the key Christian leaders in the area to attend. Then he did something he had never done before—he asked all the men to bring their wives along.

During the meeting Tao Li and his wife openly told the others about their marriage crisis and how God had helped them. Shiao Hua stood up and spoke for herself. "I believed," she explained, "that our marriage was beyond repair, and I had resolved to ask for a divorce."

As she looked around the room, she realized to her amazement that every person there was weeping. Every couple present had experienced similar pain and struggle. And every couple had hidden it so well that no one knew.

"We were able to encourage each other to be strong in the Lord," Shiao Hua told one of our Chinese colleagues later, "and to help each other become better husbands and wives. Of course, it's only a beginning. But it helps us to find a balance between ministry and family."

During a later conversation with that same Chinese colleague, I asked the question that had been on my heart all along. "Tell me something. Is it really necessary for husbands like Tao Li to be away from home so much?"

The woman looked at me a little blankly. "What else can they do?"

"Oh, I know it's one thing when somebody is arrested and put in prison—that's beyond anybody's control," I answered. "And I know that God provides strength according to the weight of the cross he asks us to carry—he's promised to do that. But why can't couples who are serving the Lord in China spend more time together?"

The woman looked at me thoughtfully. "Things are very different in the West," she said. "And maybe we can learn from each other. One of the Christian leaders told us that there should never be a conflict in God's calling. We are called to serve God but also to serve each other in our families. So many husbands feel guilty because they have not been good husbands. But the same is true for the wives. They admit that they have been much better at scolding than at encouraging their husbands. All I can say is that I praise the Lord that whatever our circumstances we can always start all over with God."

I nodded. "It's never too late."

That's one of the biggest lessons I learned from talking to Tao Li and Shiao Hua. With God, it's never too late.

# AH JU

THE GOD OF THE BANYAN TREE

One day as I opened my mail, I found a letter from one of our colleagues who travels extensively in Asia. He often visits the outlying areas of China and reports back to us about the progress of the Christians there and the situations that need our prayers.

"I know you're interested in wives who suffer because of their faith," he wrote. "The enclosed story is true. It's an unusual twist on a theme that is very familiar to you. I hope you enjoy it as much as I did."

As I read, I could well imagine the rural countryside—the rice paddies, the tidy villages, the ancient superstitions that still hold unbelievers in their grasp. I could envision a little hamlet where hardworking Chinese peasants struggle to make a living, where they find their greatest joy in their families. It was in just such a place that Ah Ju lived.

## CHAPTER 6

Call upon me and come and pray to me, and I will listen to you. You will seek me and find me when you seek me with all your heart.

*Jeremiah 29:12-13*

A Chinese peasant woman in her early thirties, Ah Ju had a charming smile and a strong, healthy body. As a child she had been a fun-loving free spirit. But nowadays she was always sad. Because of their country's one-child policy, children are very precious to the Chinese. And although they had been married for thirteen years, Ah Ju and her husband had never had a child.

In their part of China, the worship of local gods and of ancestors was very common, and Ah Ju continually pleaded with various village gods. Tearfully she'd ask, "Why am I barren and cursed? What have I done? Take pity on me and give me a child." But no matter how she prayed or what folklore remedies she used, she simply could not get pregnant.

For her husband, Ye Ziqin, being childless was more than a disappointment; it was a disgrace. And he felt that disgrace more keenly than anyone outside their home knew. He beat Au Ju every few days, growing angrier and angrier as he rained blows down on her small body,

"Why haven't you given me a son, you miserable cow?" he'd yell at her.

"Please, *please*—don't hit me again," Au Ju screamed, crawling away from him, sobbing helplessly in the corner of the house. For hours she would be afraid to move, curling into a ball on the floor, cowering while the tears ran into her mouth, salty and hot. Ye Ziqin also invented ways of humiliating his wife, refusing to give her the money she needed to buy food, then beating her for not cooking a proper meal for him.

In the center of the village stood a banyan—a vast, ancient tree that was believed to have healing powers. Stories about the tree abounded. One legend said the tree was a god because over two hundred years before a family had prayed to it and their crippled child had been healed. Ever since, the local people had kept an altar under the tree, dedicating babies there and lighting joss sticks when anyone was ill. With its tangle of roots and its immense, drooping branches, the old tree had become an object of worship.

One day Ah Ju took her problem to the banyan. She settled herself on her knees under its massive trunk, which split into two huge branches just above her head and spread out for fifty feet on either side. She placed an apple and two oranges on a plate, stacked another apple on top, and lit ten incense sticks. Rising to her feet, she began to wave two candles in the air. As she moved reverently around the trunk she chanted, "God of the banyan tree, place life in my womb. Give me a son!"

Afterward, she arose and looked closely at the trunk of the tree. At first she thought her eyes were deceiving her because the black, knobby trunk was wrapped in younger branches coiling around it like snakes. But one part of the tree, just higher than her head, looked like a face. And on that special day, the face seemed to be smiling at her.

Ah Ju rubbed her eyes. Was the tree really alive? She reached out to touch it, almost expecting to feel warm tissue, but it was cool under her hand. When she withdrew her palm, it was covered with blackened moss. She licked it, tasting the brackish soot from the altar fires. All at once a huge wave of hope surged into her heart.

"I'm going to have a baby!" she cried again and again.

People who lived near the tree came running out of their houses in alarm. But when they saw Ah Ju, her face was wreathed in joy.

"The tree smiled at me," she explained. "I know I'm going to get what I asked for. I'm going to have a son!"

Skeptical, but not wanting to offend the tree god, the villagers simply stared at the woman in silence.

"The god of the banyan tree has heard my prayers!" Ah Ju congratulated herself as she walked toward her house, a new lightness in her step. Once she got home, she insisted that her family come and give thanks at the tree. Even Ye Ziqin joined in, but he cautioned her sourly, "This is your last chance. If this doesn't work, I'm divorcing you!"

Two months later Ah Ju was pregnant. And, of course, there was great rejoicing in the village, and for more reasons than one. Ah Ju's good news had spread to the surrounding area, and now throngs of people were coming to worship at the banyan tree, bringing extra business to the village.

Of course Ah Ju knew what she had to do—she would have to find a way to thank the god of the banyan tree. One night, as an act of devotion, she knelt in worship beside the tree's trunk. All at once a storm descended on the village. Lightning cracked, and a sudden torrent of rain burst upon the tree. Ah Ju sheltered herself under the banyan tree as best she could, soaked, shivering, and frightened. Then came another loud crack, and a smack against her forehead. She touched her face and saw blood on her fingers.

Quaking with fear, Ah Ju looked up at the banyan tree. Instead of a smiling face, she could see only a dark, bulging trunk. As it glistened in the rain, the small wrapping branches seemed to hiss like snakes, the black knobs shifting to form a hideous gargoyle. She ran in horror from the tree.

*Why is the god of the banyan tree angry with me?* she asked herself as she fled.

Ah Ju told no one what happened to her. But in the depths of her heart she began to wonder, *What kind of child will I have from that god?* A few days later—perhaps because of the storm and the terror it caused—while hard at work in the fields, she miscarried. Again, no one knew but her.

Where the hope of a baby had been, now Ah Ju was filled with despair. She didn't dare go back to the banyan tree. Just as acutely, she dreaded going home. One day she began to walk. She wandered far away, a day's journey from her village. Her feet ached, her body shook with exhaustion, and she had no idea where she was. As she passed a small house, a friendly old lady watched her from the doorway.

"You look tired, dear," she called out. "Come in and rest awhile."

Wearily, Ah Ju went into the elderly woman's house. She noticed a small red cross on the lintel of the door as she entered.

She was surprised to find herself in the midst of some kind of a meeting. A crowd of people had gathered in the room, and one of them was reading from an old book. The language sounded very archaic to her ears, and she couldn't follow the words very well. But all at once, a phrase jolted into her body like an electric shock: ". . . and God opened her womb."

She was in a Christian house church, and the Scripture reading for the day was from the Old Testament. It was the story of Hannah—the barren woman who prayed to God and gave birth to Samuel the prophet.

Ah Ju burst into tears, sobbing loudly and uncontrollably. Alarmed, the others crowded around her. Unable to resist their compassion, she sobbed out her story, explaining as best she could all that had happened.

"For some reason," she concluded, "the god of the banyan tree is angry with me."

At that moment the old woman said something so startling, so revolutionary, that Ah Ju couldn't believe her ears.

"Then the god of the banyan tree is a very bad god," the old woman announced.

"Pardon me?" Ah Ju said in disbelief.

The old woman shook her head and carefully explained to Ah

Ju that the people in her home worshiped a supreme God, a God of all gods who is kind and loving and unchanging.

"Our God is not fickle," the old woman explained. "He wouldn't bless you one day and curse you the next."

Although her mind was spinning with questions, Ah Ju left the house strangely at peace. She felt as if a new power had entered her.

The next night Ah Ju crept out in the dark and found her way to the banyan tree. Her heart pounded in her ears, and the pressure in her chest was so severe that she was afraid her rib cage would explode. But Ah Ju steadied herself, reached up, and broke off a branch of the tree. She knew it was sacrilegious to harm the tree in any way, but Ah Ju was angry. "You miserable god!" she said. "I'm going to pray to another, more powerful god than you."

Two months later she was pregnant again.

Eight months later she gave birth prematurely to a baby boy. Ah Ju was the only one who knew that her son was premature. Everyone else thought he was the baby she had first conceived, born overdue. She had told no one about her miscarriage or about her prayer to her new God—a prayer that was sure to get her into immediate trouble with the local villagers.

Once the baby had safely arrived, Ah Ju's mother said, "We'd better go give thanks to the god of the banyan tree for giving you a son." Dutifully, her husband, parents, and sister all went to the tree with the new baby boy. The other villagers gathered around and watched the special celebration. Everyone knew that Ah Ju was the one who had revived the cult of the banyan tree. And there she was with the baby that confirmed the tree's power.

Her relatives all began to worship. They prayed, lit incense sticks, and moved in procession around and around the tree trunk, burning paper offerings. Then they noticed Ah Ju was standing apart, not participating.

"What's the matter?" they asked her. "Don't you want to give thanks to the god who gave you a son?"

She desperately wanted to tell them, but she couldn't. She was too scared, so she just stood there.

The celebratory mood suddenly changed. Her father said, "If you don't worship, this god may get angry and send demons to torment us."

Still she refused.

Finally her husband came up to her and said, "If you do not worship this god, you will never see your son again."

Slowly, she shuffled toward the banyan tree. As she reached the trunk, she bowed down. The sighs of relief from her watching relatives were audible. But they quickly turned to shrieks of horror as Au Ju courageously reached up and, grabbing another branch, broke it off. She wheeled around, brandishing it above her head, shouting, "This god gave me a son, then took him away. I worship a greater God. He gave me our son, and he is love—he won't take him back!"

Everyone thought Ah Ju had lost her mind. The village spiritual leader ordered that she be confined to her house. The baby was placed in the care of Ah Ju's mother, and Ye Ziqin made arrangements for a divorce.

But then Ah Ju had an idea. One day while everyone was working, she sneaked out and appealed her case to the local Communist Party boss, who took an interest in her story. Wishing to stamp out what he viewed as "feudal superstitions," he banned all veneration of the banyan tree and arrested her husband, putting him in jail for three months.

He also reunited Ah Ju with her son.

For Ah Ju, her husband's sentence passed far too quickly. Before long, Ye Ziqin was released from prison, having served his term. Ah Ju was gripped with fear, wondering if she should flee with the boy. She knew very well that her husband would be murderous with rage since it was her fault that he had been arrested. She strongly considered fleeing to the old woman who had helped her before.

Instead, against what seemed to be her better judgment, an inner voice told Ah Ju to stay home. Somehow she found the strength to obey.

The day arrived, the hours flew by, and Ah Ju tried to talk to the God of all gods, asking for protection and help. All at once the front door flew open. Ah Ju barely had the courage to look up at her husband. But she did. And, to her amazement, as Ye Ziqin came through the door, he stopped and smiled. It was the first time he had smiled at Ah Ju in years.

She stared at him in disbelief. Before she could ask him why he seemed so happy, he began to explain, "Ah Ju, something wonderful happened to me in jail. I met a man in prison who introduced me to a God called Jesus Christ. . . ."

# ESTHER BIRAL

## "GREAT IS THY FAITHFULNESS"

Asia is a colorful continent of myriad cultures, dramatically beautiful scenery, and people attired in every imaginable costume and style. There are countless religions in Asia, and Christianity is represented in every country. In many places the persecution of Christians is also present.

CHAPTER

If I preach voluntarily I have a reward. . . . What then is my reward? Just this: that in preaching the gospel I may offer it free of charge.

*1 Corinthians 9:17-18*

In nations like China and Vietnam, persecutors of Christians are often acting in cooperation with Communist regimes that refuse to tolerate anyone who pledges allegiance to a higher authority. Places like the Philippines are far different. Scores of religions abound there, and although Communist guerrilla groups may be responsible for some unpleasant incidents, more likely sources of trouble for Christians are militant Muslims.

In 1998 Johan and I were thoroughly enjoying a visit to the southern Philippines. For us, everything was reminiscent of Vietnam. The women's long skirts looked much like those worn by the tribal women in Vietnam—women like K'Sup Nri. The friendly faces, the warm welcomes, the weather, and the food all brought back delightful memories.

I hoped to talk to some of the Christian women who served the Lord in the Philippines. I had heard stories of Muslim converts who had become evangelists, of widows who were leading Bible studies in their homes, and of mothers whose sons had been martyred for their faith. I had been told about violent mob scenes, false legal accusations, and death threats. I longed to talk to women whose experiences would help us in the West better understand and more effectively pray for them.

# A Husband's Answered Prayer

Johan and I attended a Layleaders Training Institute in Zamboanga, a city on the island of Mindanao. Our second day there a hot humid breeze lazily rustled in the trees, and not a cloud could be seen in the brilliant tropical sky. Just as our session was finished, an Open Doors colleague called me aside.

"There's a woman I'd like you to meet," he said. "I think you may have heard about her story—her house was burned down. Do you remember?"

"Oh yes, I do."

After being properly introduced, I found myself looking into the face of a woman whose dignity and poise profoundly impressed me. Esther Biral had a serious, thoughtful manner yet was quick to smile. Like most Filipino Christians, her enthusiasm for the Lord was tremendous. And once she began to tell me her story, I could see that it was a lesson in faith and forgiveness.

"I was raised in a very influential Muslim family," Esther told me. "My parents came from families of Imams—Muslim teachers—and they were both very well respected in our community."

At a young age Esther had learned to read from the Koran in Arabic. She even knew how to chant verses from the Koran, which not many people in her community were able to do. Islam in her region of the Philippines was often mingled with superstitious folk beliefs. As a result, Muslim missionaries began to arrive from countries like Pakistan and Libya to teach pure Islam in the islands of Sulu and Tawi Tawi.

"Before I was twenty years old," Esther continued with a smile, "my life changed dramatically. My family arranged for me to marry a widower, who was a distant relative. He was fifteen years older than I, and he had become a Christian when he was a teenager."

"Your parents arranged for you to marry a *Christian?*" Disbelief must have been written across my face. "Johan and I have visited countries in the Middle East, where a man could be sentenced to the death penalty for such a thing!"

Esther laughed at my shocked outburst. "No, things aren't quite that rigid here. Somehow family ties and tradition are stronger than religious laws. At least they used to be."

So Esther married the Christian man. Thanks to her parents, she was very dogmatic in her beliefs and determined to remain a Muslim. She made that very clear to her husband. And he made it very clear to her that he would love her no matter what she believed.

"He never forced me to become a Christian," Esther assured me. "He would never do that. Instead, it was his loving attitude toward me and a miracle from God that finally won me to Christ."

"What kind of miracle?"

Esther and her husband, Alex, for the most part were genuinely happy newlyweds. Like all husbands and wives, they had their differences, but Alex was an exceptionally kind man, and he treated his wife with such high regard that they seldom found reason to raise their voices in anger or disagreement. Peace and tranquility reigned in their home.

But there was one enormous problem: Esther was plagued with miscarriages. No matter how careful she was, no matter how zealously she protected herself, she kept losing her babies before they were born. And every time it happened, it broke her heart.

Finally, after their fourth miscarriage, Alex sat beside Esther on the bed where she was resting and took her hand in his. She was still feeling weakened by the loss of blood, and she was weeping inconsolably, her eyes swollen with tears. Alex's heart went out to her.

"Would you mind if I prayed for you?" he asked quietly.

She shrugged. "I don't care." Muslims believe in prayer. And besides, what more did she have to lose?

"Lord Jesus," Alex prayed, "I thank you for sending your only begotten Son into the world. It's in his name that I come to you now on behalf of my precious wife. Lord, she has suffered so much in her efforts to bring a child into our family. And today, once again, her heart is aching over the loss of yet another baby. Lord Jesus, would you heal her body? Would you please give her the child she wants so much to carry in her arms? We will give you all the praise and honor for your help. And we will accept your will no matter what happens. Thank you, Lord. In Jesus' name, amen."

For the next few minutes Alex wiped Esther's tears and held her in his arms to comfort her. And somehow she felt an unusual peace in her heart.

Within weeks she was pregnant again, and this time, despite her doubts and fears, the baby continued to grow. She passed the second month, passed the third month, and soon realized that she had remained pregnant longer than ever before.

In due time the couple's first baby was born, healthy and whole. Nine more children would follow.

"Alex," Esther told her husband as she held her firstborn son in her arms, "I'm so grateful for this child. I know Jesus gave him to me, and I want to follow Jesus, too."

## MUSLIM-BACKGROUND BELIEVER

Esther prayed with Alex to receive Jesus into her life. From that day on, she stopped going to the mosque. She was, once and for all, a Christian convert, known as a *kafir* among Muslims. Because of this, Esther was soon faced with real opposition from her family.

In fact, it wasn't just the family's practice of Islam that troubled Esther. As she studied the Word of God, she learned that it is wrong to worship anything or anyone apart from him. So besides rejecting her former Muslim beliefs, she also refused to worship the spirits of her ancestors any longer. That created problems with even more members of her family.

"You are a disgrace!" an elderly aunt shouted at her one day. "Don't you think I prayed to my gods for your child to be born? How can you turn against the faith of your relatives and accept a foreign belief?"

"Faith in Jesus is not a foreign belief, Auntie," Esther explained. "There are other Christians in our village—"

"I don't care who's in our village! You're a disgrace to us all!"

Naturally, the reaction of the Muslim relatives was no less intense. Since her Islamic background had included comprehensive teaching from authorities in the Koran, Esther knew very well the differences between Islam and Christianity. There was no compromise possible. But difficult as it was for her to defy the traditions of her family, she did not waver. With her husband and other Christians she diligently studied the Bible. This provided the spiritual nourishment she needed to grow strong and healthy in her newfound faith.

Esther's husband had a regular job in the post office. But for him and Esther, church involvement and ministry soon became the center of their lives. Their primary vocation was to provide leadership for the Christians in their mostly Muslim village. Because Alex was so busy, much of the visiting and ministry work was left to Esther. And she was happy to help—it gave her great pleasure to support her husband's Christian service. But, of course, it isn't a particularly easy matter to be a Christian pastor's wife in a Muslim community. In fact, it can be more than difficult—it can be dangerous.

Esther quickly learned that Christian children sometimes have a more difficult time than their parents. Christian children know that they aren't supposed to retaliate, even though they are sometimes taunted, teased, and tormented by Muslim children. Esther often found herself consoling her children—especially the little ones—because of unkind words or cruel blows. It broke her heart to bandage their wounds and to wipe away their tears. How she longed for the day when they would be old enough to understand that their faith really was worthy of all the suffering.

The Christian families in the community encouraged their children to play with each other, and that relieved some of the stress. But there was always a sense of slight discomfort in their homes. An edginess. An uncertainty. Every Christian in a Muslim community knows that trouble can break out at any time.

One night Esther awoke from a sound sleep. Outside the house she saw a strange glow and heard a roaring sound. One look at the window told her that the whole village seemed to be on fire.

The Biral family rushed down from their house, which was constructed on stilts, and into the street.

"What happened? How did it start?" Alex asked a neighbor.

"Your guess is as good as mine! Nobody knows anything," the neighbor answered, squinting into the blaze.

Everyone watched in silence as raging flames engulfed several houses. Fortunately, the Biral house was spared.

Then, a few nights later, two of Esther's children rushed

inside. "Mom, we saw a man pouring gasoline outside our house! He just ran away!"

Again Esther herded the children outside. Again they smelled the smoke and heard the sound of the inferno. This time, however, their home was not spared. It was the only one burning. The Birals fled, looking back to see flames licking up the sides of the house and the stilts collapse as the entire wooden structure was consumed. No one was hurt, but everything in the house was lost.

## Faith and Forgiveness

"Why would anyone do that?" I asked Esther. "Was is because you are Christians?"

She looked into my eyes without the slightest trace of anger on her face. "We never found out who did it or why, and we will never know for sure. But, as a family, we've left it with the Lord. He tells us to forgive."

Then Esther proudly showed me photographs of the new house Open Doors had helped provide for the Biral family. Like the other, it, too, was constructed of wood and built on stilts. I was shocked to realize that there were just two rooms for twelve people. How could such a large family live in such a small house? *These are poor people*, I reminded myself. It was hard to remember that in the face of Esther's remarkable grace and dignity.

She had lost every material possession she owned, but Esther had no complaints. Instead, she was counting her blessings. Yes, poverty was a constant problem. Yes, it would be nice to have a bit more money—it was difficult to make ends meet.

"But the Lord is so good to us," she said. And her smile lit up the room. "Did you know that our daughter Ruth is in her third year at Ebenezer Bible College? We're so proud of her! She wants to become a missionary." Esther went on to tell me how excited she and her husband were about several young people in their community who had just received Christ.

Knowing how dangerous it is in many countries to convert from Islam to Christianity, I asked, "What advice do you give to your new converts. How do you teach them to follow Jesus?"

"Jesus told us to go into all the world and preach the gospel," Esther pointed out. And 'all the world' includes our Muslim neighbors. We do advise new believers to keep a low profile for a while, not to be too vocal about their new faith right away so they can grow stronger. Opposition will undoubtedly come—we can't prevent that. It comes to all of us. But God is faithful. He is *always* faithful."

On our final day in Zamboanga, Johan spoke at a meeting at Ebenezer Bible College. Tears filled my eyes as Esther and her husband, together with about twenty to thirty other Muslim-background believers, formed a choir and sang a beautiful old hymn.

Great is Thy faithfulness, O God my Father,
There is no shadow of turning with Thee. . . .
All I have needed Thy hand hath provided—
Great is Thy faithfulness, Lord, unto me!

Esther Biral is a woman of great faithfulness, and God has been wonderfully faithful to her. It seems to me that God is especially faithful to those who suffer great loss for following his beloved Son.

# PURIFICACIÓN AND JOY

## "I AM NOT AFRAID"

Purificación Bagtasos stood proudly at her husband's side, smiling at her friends and enjoying the warm Philippine sun. It was a balmy, pleasant Sunday, and John had just preached a powerful sermon at their morning worship service. It gave Purificación great delight to see her husband happy, and he was never happier than on Sunday morning. It was then that the members of their little congregation gathered and celebrated the Lord's Day together.

CHAPTER 8

They were just about to head home to share a meal with several other families when a police car pulled up outside the church. A solemn looking officer got out and walked toward them. The crowd fell silent.

God is faithful; he will not let you be tempted beyond what you can bear. But when you are tempted, he will also provide a way out so that you can stand up under it.

*1 Corinthians 10:13*

## BAD NEWS FROM ALAT

"I'm looking for Mr. and Mrs. Bagtasos," he explained. "Do you know where I might find them?"

"I'm Pastor Bagtasos, and this is my wife. How can we help you?"

"Do you have a son named Severino?"

Purificación's heart began to pound. Her husband protectively put his arm around her.

"Yes, Severino is our son. He is a pastor on Jolo Island. Why do you ask?"

The officer, who was a young man with little experience at such things, simply said, "He's dead. He's been murdered."

The people caught their breath. Several of the women began to cry.

"Are you sure it is our son?" Pastor Bagtasos asked quietly. "Do you have any other details?"

"He was shot. That's all I know. It happened earlier today. Sorry to bring you such terrible news, sir."

"Thank you for coming," Pastor Bagtasos said, extending his hand. "I'm sure it wasn't easy for you."

The crowd began to disperse. Some of the Bagtasos's closest friends gathered around, embracing them and praying quietly with them.

"You always know deep down that something like this can happen," Purificación murmured through her tears. "But when it does . . ."

"You're never really prepared," her husband said, holding her close to him.

"I just can't quite believe it. Maybe there's some mistake."

But subsequent calls confirmed the worst. Severino, or "Junie" as his family called him, was indeed dead. He had been murdered because of his Christian faith.

In the hours and days that followed, the Bagtasos began to ask themselves the kinds of questions parents anywhere would have. Why had God allowed it? What was his purpose?

They told each other again and again, "The Lord knows best." Yet their hearts were broken.

During those early hours when they struggled with the loss of their son, Purificación said to her husband, "We just have to believe that God did not change his character when our son died. He is still a good and faithful Father, and we know we can trust him."

"I know, my love, by it doesn't keep my heart from aching."

The following day the grieving couple set out for Alat, where Severino's father would preach the sermon at his son's memorial service. "You never expect to outlive your children," he said sadly. "It's a hard thing to face." But face it they did, and with great dignity.

When they arrived at their son's church, the Bagtasos realized that the murderer—or people who were involved in the murder—just might be there. They looked around, wondering who was present.

As Pastor Bagtasos concluded his message, he said, "I want you to know that we forgive you, but we will not stop sharing about Christ. There are four more preachers in our family. If you want us to stop preaching the gospel, you will have to come and kill us, too."

Two years later, as the sun spangled across the blue waters of the Celebes Sea, Johan and I made our way to the chapel at Ebenezer Bible College. On the path leading to the church we noticed a couple walking alongside us.

Our colleague Pete greeted them warmly, then said to us, "Please meet Mr. and Mrs. Bagtasos." Somehow, their name sounded familiar. After a moment of concentration, I remembered.

"Are you Severino's parents?"

"We are . . . ," the woman said with a smile.

I'm so glad to meet you!" I said warmly, reaching out to shake their hands. "I feel like I know you."

## LOVE AND LOSS

In January 1996 the sad news of Severino Bagtasos's murder had reached us. Jolo Island, where he died, is a Muslim-dominated area in the southern Philippines. And although the news had shocked us, after we heard the details, we realized it was probably more of a surprise to us than it had been to Junie.

Severino Bagstasos decided to follow Jesus at a young age. One of eleven children, he was always grateful to have grown up in a loving Christian family.

His father's church was located on one of the islands of the Sulu Archipelago. Populated mostly by Muslims, it has seen many years of violent religious conflict. Along with two brothers and a sister, Severino felt called to the ministry. He followed his older sister, Joy, to study at Ebenezer Bible college in Zamboanga City.

The years in Bible college were a happy time for Severino. He felt privileged to be able to study the Word of God, learn how to lead a church, and share the gospel with unbelievers. His classes provided excellent preparation for the future, but he especially enjoyed the fun and fellowship with other students.

One day a lively young woman caught his attention. Like Junie's sister, her name was Joy—Joy Dimerin. Like her name, she radiated the exuberance and a love for life that only the Lord can give. It wasn't long before the two of them were inseparable.

After his graduation Severino was assigned to pastor the Christian and Missionary Alliance church in Alat on the island of Jolo. Under his leadership the church prospered. Nothing made Severino happier than to see new people joining his congregation, and he longed to share this pleasure with Joy. Besides, he felt rather lonely living in a house by himself and often thought that life would be much better if he and Joy were able to minister as a couple. He had seen that kind of ministry partnership in his own home, and he wanted it for himself.

"Joy," he told her one day, "my mother has been such a blessing to so many people. I know you would be the same kind of pastor's wife that she is. But more than that, I just can't imagine life without you. Will you marry me?"

"Of course I'll marry you!" she cried. "I love you."

Severino could hardly wait for Joy to join him. It would not be long now before she graduated. The date for their wedding was set for May 23, 1998.

Besides his loving commitment to his own congregation, Severino also had a passion for reaching out into the local Muslim community. He distributed tracts and conducted home Bible studies that included some interested Muslims. It didn't take him long to learn that this particular kind of evangelism could be very dangerous indeed.

"If you don't stop trying to make us change our faith, we'll kill you!" he was told in no uncertain terms. In fact, he was threatened on several occasions. But this did not stop Severino; he didn't even hesitate.

"Jesus said that we should go into all the world and preach the gospel," he told his friends. "This island is part of that world, and people need to hear the Good News." Naturally, for him, "all the world" included his Muslim friends and neighbors.

One Sunday morning as he looked across his congregation, Severino was touched to see a member of the *Tablig*, a group of itinerant Muslim evangelists, in church. Severino had befriended the young man, and on several occasions he had shared the gospel with him. In turn, the Muslim evangelist had tried to convince Severino that he should join the Islamic faith and become a member of the Tablig. Severino often prayed that the Lord would reveal himself to this zealous young friend of his. But later the relationship had somehow broken down, and the two young men stopped having their friendly discussions.

Then Severino received an anonymous letter. "If you will resist from joining us," it said, "then we advise you to stop what you are doing in your church. If you refuse, then something will happen to you, and your life will be shortened."

Severino was shocked. For the first time he realized that this was serious business. Anxious and shaken, he brought the letter before the Lord. As he prayed he was well aware that the writers of the letter probably meant every word they had written. His life was in danger, but he could choose between life and death. Was he willing to lay down his life? Or was he going to react in fear of those who could kill the body but not the soul?

The young man struggled for hours. He spent a sleepless night before the Lord. "God," he prayed as he tossed and turned, "what do you want me to do? Am I being foolhardy in trying to reach these people for you? I need your wisdom, Lord!"

Gradually, through the course of the night, peace filled Severino's heart. He knew what he had to do. By morning the choice had been made: He would obey God rather than men.

Severino decided not to talk about the letter—he knew people would be worried, and some of them might encourage him to change his mind. He did, however, confide in one of his friends. "If I'm killed," Severino told him, "so be it. I am ready to die for Jesus. But if I have to be killed, I would prefer to die in the church doing the Lord's work."

The next Sunday morning Severino's sister Joy, who had come to help him in his ministry, was preaching in his church on the topic of heaven. Severino was sitting in the front pew, listening to her conclude her message when suddenly a lone gunman moved stealthily forward from the back of the church. There were two loud pops, and several people screamed. The gunman fired two bullets at

Severino. One bullet passed through his cheek; the other through his chest.

"I thought the gunshots were the sound of firecrackers. Hecklers sometimes throw them into the church to interrupt us," Severino's sister told me.

"So didn't you see the stranger come into the church?"

"Yes, but we all thought he was just a latecomer. Only after I saw my brother's body slump to the ground did I realize what had happened."

"Did anybody run after the killer?"

"We were all so shocked, we were almost paralyzed," Joy recalled. "The murderer was able to get away and to this day hasn't been found."

According to a church leader from the area, the simple act of passing out a gospel tract could have instigated the shooting since that very day was the start of Ramadan, the Muslim period of fasting. Some Muslim sects believe that if you kill an enemy of Allah on the first day of Ramadan, the act will ensure your passage into paradise.

## DEALING WITH HEARTBREAK

So now I was finally face-to-face with Severino's parents—faithful ministers of the gospel themselves. "The Lord has used the death of our son," Purificación said as she smiled. "Now a number of Muslims have seen that Jesus is real in our lives. Many have come in secret to ask us and our children questions about our faith."

*How can she find the strength to look at her son's murder that way?* I thought, trying to imagine how I would respond to the brutal slaying of one of my children.

"How did you cope with your grief?" I asked her.

"Well, it certainly hasn't been easy. But the prayers of Christians all over the world have carried us through. We've received so many cards and letters. Even this past Christmas, almost two years after our son was killed, we still received greetings from all around the world."

Intrigued by the sweetness of this mother and the peace and joy that she exuded, I wanted to hear more from her.

"Haven't you felt angry at God for allowing this to happen?" In our Western culture, God so often gets the blame when anything bad happens. How many times had I heard people say after a tragedy occurred, "Where is God now? If he is so almighty, why didn't he prevent this?"

But that kind of response never occurred to the Bagtasos. "Angry with God? Oh no, not at all." Nor did their open, friendly faces betray any anger. These were not bitter people. Instead, their faith had been deepened and purified through intense testing. "How could we be angry with God? He's the one who carried us through." Purificación seemed almost puzzled by my question. "Where would we be without his comfort?"

Just then Pete, our colleague, reluctantly interrupted. "Sorry, but we have to go now; the meeting is starting." I had almost forgotten we were on our way to another gathering. Having a chance to talk to the Bagtasos had been such an unexpected, pleasant surprise.

## Joy in the Midst of Pain

While Johan was speaking in chapel, I found it difficult to concentrate on what he was saying. Though I had not met her, I kept thinking of Joy Dimerin. Severino's death was a huge loss to her as well. My thoughts went back to November 12, 1968, when I said good-bye to my own fiancé for a year as he served the missionaries in Vietnam.

During Johan's commissioning service Brother Andrew said that we had no guarantee in the Bible that Johan would return. "God only commands us to go, he does not say anything about coming back," he concluded.

I've heard Andrew say those words many more times in the years since, but never have they cut into my soul as deeply as they did that day. At the time, because of the Vietnam War, the possibility of Johan not returning was very real. And I could not bear the thought of it. I could hardly imagine how Joy had faced the terrible news about Severino.

I did not meet Joy Dimerin, but I did talk to her parents. I learned that she, too, had also spoken at Junie's funeral. What a difficult day it had been for her. Instead of making preparations for her wedding, she had to say good-bye forever to her handsome and beloved fiancé.

"Though I am suffering deeply," she explained to those who attended the funeral, "I can still praise the Lord. The worst threats could not stop my fiancé from serving the Lord. May God forgive the man who killed him. May he see Jesus Christ. Junie, till we meet again in heaven . . ."

God drew near to Joy in her intense pain. In a letter of thanks to those who supported her in her grief, she wrote,

Being brokenhearted for two years led me to spiritual wholeness. Your prayers and encouragement helped me to be faithful to my Lord and Redeemer, and also to be committed to whatever task he will entrust me with.

Throughout those years, God has been teaching me not to look on the pain and hurts as though he is being unjust, unloving, or ungracious. Instead, to view these things as his molding process for me to be strong and firm, and also to consider it for my own good (Romans 8:28).

God is teaching me not to scoff at him whenever I'm in pain or suffering. For he's the one who can deliver me. He knows what is best for me. If, through suffering and pain his purpose and will be fulfilled, may it be done.

God is teaching me that he does not allow suffering that I cannot bear. Indeed, I can (1 Cor. 10:13)! For God's grace always abounds. God will give me the unique grace to bear my unique cross.

God is teaching me that suffering and pain do not come from him but from the enemy (James 1:13). With God's permissive will, he allows it for his purpose and glory.

For my coworkers in the Lord, remember God's promise is clear that those who wait for him in their suffering will receive strength and endurance that others know nothing about.

Joy graduated from Ebenezer Bible College in Zamboanga, and she is presently involved in the work of Love Your Neighbor—a ministry that seeks to bring the gospel of Jesus to Muslims in the southern Philippines.

## "PLEASE PRAY AGAINST DISCOURAGEMENT"

Before we left Asia, I had one more opportunity to meet with Purificación. And there was one question I really needed to ask her. "How can we pray for you? Are you concerned about the safety of your other children in ministry?" I asked. "Are you afraid that something might happen to your husband?"

"No," she answered. "Fear is not my main prayer request. I'm not afraid. But please pray that we won't get discouraged. It really hurts us to see so many young people leaving our area to go and study somewhere else. There is a lot of poverty here. It is hard for them to make a living. I'm afraid that before too long we will only have old ladies left in our church.

"We also need discernment and wisdom in ministering to Muslims. It is often a one-on-one ministry done in secret. We find that many Muslims are open to the gospel—especially after Junie's death."

As we said good-bye, she took my hand and thanked Johan and me again for our prayers and support during the time of their great loss.

"Please thank all the people who prayed for us and sent us cards. Please tell them the Lord has answered their prayers. Our hearts have found comfort in the Lord and in the love of believers from all around the world."

Purificación will probably never know how much she ministered to me. She reminded me again that it is safe to entrust our children to our loving heavenly Father's care. She was also a vibrant example of the power of forgiveness. Her shining face showed no trace of bitterness because she had been able to forgive even the murderer of her son. If she could forgive something as serious as that, shouldn't I be able to forgive those who hurt me or my family members—intentionally or unintentionally? That forgiving spirit had set Purificación free, and it allowed the Lord to continue to use her.

I couldn't get the Bagtasos family out of my mind in the days that followed. I thought about them all, but especially Purificación and Joy. What fitting names for those dear sisters. Tested by the fire, Purificación had indeed come out purified, shining like the finest gold, reflecting the Savior she loves so well. And Joy continues to allow the Lord to shine through her, for his joy is her strength.

# MIDDLE
# EAST

# TAKOOSH HOVSEPIAN

## IN GOD'S UNIVERSITY

Takoosh was a lively Iranian teenager from an Armenian background with flashing dark eyes and a beautiful smile. She sometimes attended church with her grandmother, and there she heard that she could have a personal relationship with Jesus Christ. For some reason, she just couldn't get the idea out of her mind, and after several conversations she prayed with some of her friends and invited the Lord into her life.

CHAPTER 9

Soon after she came to Jesus, Takoosh brought a very important request to God in prayer. "Lord, please give me a husband who loves you. I want so much to serve you, and I pray for a partner who is a Christian so that we can serve you together."

Of course she had no way of knowing that a young man named Haik Hovsepian was bringing a very similar request before God. Haik was a believer, too. He had just finished his studies and felt he was being called by God into Christian ministry.

"Lord," he prayed, "I want you to use me in your service. But I need someone to stand with me, someone to share my ministry with me. Please help me find a godly girl who wants to please you above all else. Lead me to her, Lord, and I'll ask her to be my wife."

> Praise be to the God and Father of our Lord Jesus Christ, the Father of compassion and the God of all comfort, who comforts us in all our troubles, so that we can comfort those in any trouble with the comfort we ourselves have received from God."
>
> *2 Corinthians 1:3-4*

Haik often served as a guest speaker in various churches. One Sunday morning he visited the city of Isfahan. While he was preaching there, his eyes fell on a fifteen-year-old girl sitting in the audience. There were quite a few other young women sitting in the congregation, but for some reason his eyes were drawn to that one special face. He had fasted and prayed that he would find a godly wife before making the journey. Was it his imagination, or was the Lord saying, *This is the woman you have prayed for. I have chosen her for you!*

Could it be so? Or was he simply responding to a pair of dark eyes, a quiet spirit, a lovely smile? He couldn't be sure. She seemed a little too tall and slim, but something in his spirit kept saying, *This is the one.* Well aware that he was about to make one of the most important decisions of his life, Haik fasted and prayed for three days. And by the end of his fasting, he still felt that the Lord was speaking to him in the same way.

Fighting off his doubts and fears, the young man summoned all his courage and went to talk to Takoosh. He told her about his prayer for a godly wife. "This is a little hard to explain," he began rather sheepishly, "but I think God has shown me that you're the woman he has chosen for me."

Takoosh was stunned. She wasn't sure what to say, but deep in her heart she had much the same feeling. In an unsteady voice, she answered, "Like you, I've been praying for a mate who wants to serve the Lord with me. Maybe you're the answer to my prayer, too."

Later that evening, when she tried to talk things over with her parents, they weren't at all pleased. "You don't even know this man!" they protested. "And you need to finish your education. What if you're left alone some day and you have to work? You'll have nothing to fall back on!"

But the more she talked to Haik and the more she talked to God, the more Takoosh was convinced that this man really was the one for her. After much conversation with her parents and after many private prayers, Takoosh's family eventually relented. They were, in fact, impressed with the young man, too.

"He is an exceptional boy," her father said. "I can see that for myself."

## GREAT JOY, DEEP SORROW

So at quite a young age, Takoosh became Mrs. Hovsepian. She soon found out that being married to a pastor in Iran was not exactly an easy life. But Haik's love and his gentle, romantic ways helped her through the early adjustments. He clearly loved her, and they both deeply loved the Lord.

Those were days of increasing political upheaval in Iran, which eventually culminated in the 1979 Islamic Revolution. Before long, Takoosh's parents fled the country and moved to the United States.

"Are you wishing you could move to the States, too?" Haik asked her the day she told her parents good-bye.

"No," Takoosh told him. "There's no way I'm leaving you. I am staying here. But just remember—I'm doing it for you!"

"I'd rather you stayed for God," Haik countered.

But from that time on, perhaps because he was the only family she now had in the country, Haik began to treat his wife like a queen. He realized it was painful for Takoosh to live such a huge distance away from her loved ones. So he did everything he could to encourage her and keep her spirits up.

The two of them were genuinely well matched and content with one another, and their happiness was inexpressible when their first child, a little boy, was born. Like most new fathers, Haik was enormously proud of the baby. And the more Haik fell in love with their son, the more Takoosh fell in love with Haik. Those were the most joyful days of her life—caring for her infant son and watching his father's delight in him.

"God, you are so good to us," Takoosh sometimes prayed, feeling deep gratitude for her new family. "You've given me a wonderful husband who loves you and a beautiful baby. I'm so thankful that we're serving you together."

By then, Haik was pastoring a Christian fellowship, which was growing larger ever week. Not only was he an excellent Bible teacher, but Haik was also a gifted musician who loved to lead the congregation in praise. He had an exceptionally good voice, and the worship in their church never failed to move her to tears. "Thank you, Lord, for all you've done for us," Takoosh often prayed, feeling blessed in ways she never could have imagined.

Unfortunately the greatest joys in life sometimes have to make room for the deepest sorrows. And so it would be for Takoosh, who would soon have to face more than her share of suffering. One night as they drove to a Christian meeting, Haik's car was struck head-on by another vehicle. The other driver was clearly at fault, but it was little comfort to anyone. Haik and Takoosh were severely injured. Their beautiful son was killed instantly.

Takoosh's physical pain was severe, but her emotional agony was indescribable.

"How could you allow this to happen to us, Lord?" Takoosh often cried out as her body slowly and painfully mended. "All we ever wanted to do was to serve you. Why didn't you protect us? Why did our baby have to die?"

There were no easy answers for Takoosh's desperate questions, and for many months it seemed that her broken spirit would never heal. It took her a very long time to stop being angry at God. Thankfully, the other Christians in their church understood her battle, and they interceded for her continually. They prayed that Takoosh would be able to forgive the other driver. They prayed that the Lord would heal her aching heart. And they helped in every practical way imaginable.

Eventually, Takoosh relinquished her bitterness into God's hands, and once she did so, the wound in her heart gradually diminished. As time went by, she learned how to keep her sorrow in its place, especially after the Lord gave her and Haik another son.

Meanwhile, Haik was a tower of strength during this terrible time. His strong faith in God made it possible for him not to waver in days of adversity. Rather than dwelling on his own loss, he went out of his way to help Takoosh. She was amazed to see that her husband would do anything to make her life easier. Her love for him knew no bounds. He was the light of her life.

## "Brother Haik Is Missing"

Over the years, as their family increased so did their persecutions. After the death of their first son, Haik and Takoosh with blessed with four more children—three sons and a daughter. And when Mehdi Dibaj, another Iranian pastor, was taken to prison and his wife was unable to care for their children, the family increased yet again. Haik became like a father to the Dibaj children as well.

By now Haik's role in the Iranian Christian community had

become both more important and more visible. He was now chairman of the Council of Protestant Pastors. It was up to him in this position to issue a report about the violations of Christians' rights in Iran, a report that was published all over the world. He also refused to endorse a document produced by Iran's religious and political authorities stating that the Christian church in Iran enjoyed freedom of religion. This made him no friends in the hardcore fundamentalist regime that now ruled the country.

To make matters worse, when Haik was pressured to stop reaching out to Muslims with the gospel message, he flatly refused. He made it clear that his Tehran church would continue to welcome anyone and everyone who wanted to know more about Jesus the Messiah.

Brother Haik preached the gospel everywhere he went, to whomever would listen, no matter what their beliefs. No government could restrain him. His church was alive and active, and Haik was loved by everyone who knew him—everyone except the Iranian authorities. Living an outspoken Christian life in a militantly Muslim world was a challenge few believers would dare to face, but Haik faced it daily, along with other Christian leaders who shared his courage and faith. Haik set an example for the entire world to see by refusing to give in to intimidation and fear.

One day in January 1994, Haik kissed Takoosh good-bye and headed for the airport, where he was scheduled to meet with a friend. At first, when he didn't return, she thought the authorities might have detained him. But when she called around, every official said the same thing: "We don't know anything about him." Takoosh's best hope was that her husband was in jail.

A couple of days later, Johan, the children and I were starting to eat dinner when the telephone interrupted our mealtime conversation. Johan took the call, and as he listened to the voice on the other end of the phone, the expression on his face told us all that something was terribly wrong.

The call was from California, from an Iranian Christian friend there. "Johan, Brother Haik has been missing for two days. Nobody knows where he is or what's happened to him. He went to the airport to meet somebody and never returned home. Please pray, and try to mobilize others to pray as well. Frankly, it doesn't look good. . . ."

The sad news came as a shock, but it was not totally unexpected. We knew Pastor Haik had been extremely outspoken about the persecution of Iranian Christians. During the previous months, there had been a worldwide campaign to protest and pray against the imminent execution of Mehdi Dibaj, whose children Haik and Takoosh had been caring for the nine years he had been in jail. Dibaj had been unexpectedly released only a few days before.

Through Open Doors, we contacted friends and colleagues who organized a massive prayer effort. Within hours, thousands of people in dozens of countries were praying for Haik around the clock.

Finally, after more than a week of anxiously waiting for news about his whereabouts, on Sunday morning, January 30, the phone rang at the Hovsepian house. Takoosh handed the receiver to their oldest son, Joseph. "It's the police," she said quietly. "They want to talk to you."

When Joseph arrived at the police station, an officer unceremoniously thrust a grisly photograph into his hands. "Is this your father?" the policeman asked coldly. "We found this body in a small alleyway in Tehran. He was brutally murdered. Looks like he died about ten days ago."

Joseph identified the body in the photograph as his father's.

Waves of shock rippled across the world. In fact, many Christians—even those who didn't know Haik personally—felt that they had lost a close friend. But Takoosh and her four children, ages ten to twenty-three, had lost the dearest person in all the world to them.

Takoosh wept for days. The skin beneath her eyes became inflamed and infected. She simply could not stop crying. Days later our own eyes filled with tears as we watched a video of the memorial service in the Assembly of God church in Tehran. I could not take my eyes off Haik's widow. She was seated in the front row, surrounded by her children, all dressed in black. Her face was a study in tragedy. I wondered if she would ever smile again.

The church was filled to overflowing. A large picture of Haik was placed on the platform surrounded by dozens of floral wreaths and bouquets. We listened in silence to a recording of one of Haik's sermons on persecution and suffering. Later on, his beautiful voice filled the auditorium as one of his recorded songs was played.

The camera zoomed in on Mehdi Dibaj. "Not Haik, but I should have died!" he exclaimed when he spoke during the service. It wasn't long before his words proved prophetic.

## LESSONS TO BE LEARNED

Christians everywhere prayed for Takoosh and her family, and for the believers in Iran who were going through such a difficult time. Thousands of letters and cards were sent. Their greetings were appreciated, but the wound in Takoosh's spirit seemed beyond repair. As the reality of Haik's murder sank in, she found herself in a mighty spiritual struggle.

Takoosh's heart was filled with hatred toward the murderers of her husband. She hated the Muslims who had brought this tremendous grief upon her and her family. Thoughts of vindication festered in her mind. She was afraid of her own rage, afraid that she would lose control and strike someone with her car or cause injury to an innocent person.

When friends visited Takoosh some months later, she shook her head and said, "I've been in God's University. I started out in the lowest grade, but slowly and steadily he began to work in my heart. First, I simply had to be *willing* to forgive the murderers. Forgiveness started with a decision of the will, and the emotions followed much later. One day, after giving God permission to take it away, I realized that the hatred was gone. At last I could forgive the people who killed my husband."

Takoosh had won a battle, but it was not long before she became aware of another hurdle. God was asking her to not only forgive her enemies but to *love* them.

"Lord, you're asking too much," she cried out to him. "How can I love them when they killed the love of my life?"

God gently took her by the hand and helped her. Little by little, step-by-step, she came to the point where she realized that she *could* love her enemies. She began to see the Muslim extremists the way God saw them—as lost sheep without a Shepherd. God asked Takoosh to love, and he enabled her to love. He helped her to pass the second test.

"But I still wasn't quite ready to graduate from God's University," she said. "The process was not over. God told me that he wanted me to praise and thank him for what had happened."

It was impossible. Forgiveness and love she could deal with dutifully, but praise required her to sing, to rejoice, to celebrate. How could anyone expect her to do that? God knew how much Haik had meant to her, how she needed him and depended on him.

"Still, I wanted to be obedient and grow in the Lord," Takoosh explained. "So again I had no other choice. With my mouth I started to thank the Lord, even though my heart was crying at the same time. My heart was not ready, but I obeyed with my mouth. And God, as before, started to work in my soul."

The Christian men and women in the Tehran church went out of their way to help the Hovsepian family. During the days Haik was missing, and after the news of his death was confirmed, church members and many local pastors took turns in comforting Takoosh and the children.

For a long time they took care of her everyday needs in the most practical ways. They shopped, they cooked, they cleaned, they served guests. There was not a day that Takoosh was left alone. Someone was always there to comfort her, to encourage her from the Scriptures, and to provide for her.

"Though I missed my family a lot, there was not a moment after Haik's death that I wished that they were with me," Takoosh shared. "I received all the love, care, and comfort I needed from the church."

The Lord himself was real to Takoosh in personal, sometimes amazingly tangible, ways. God demonstrated to her that he was not only interested in providing for her big needs but was also concerned about the smallest details of her life. One of the little comforts Takoosh enjoyed was eating chocolate.

One day, to her regret, she realized that she had only a little piece left. As she ate it she prayed, "Please, Lord, you know how I love chocolate. Would you send me some more?"

That same day some visitors from Canada and the United

States arrived in her apartment. She gratefully unwrapped their gifts—toys and clothes for the other martyrs' families. And, then, at the very last, she joyfully opened something that had been brought especially for her—chocolate. Once again Takoosh was reminded of her heavenly Father's unfailing care.

One of the Takoosh's most difficult times was when Rebecca, their daughter, got married, Takoosh needed supernatural grace to somehow make it a joyful day for the young couple. Haik and Takoosh had been looking forward to this happy occasion together. Now she had to go through it alone. While the house was being decorated for the wedding, Takoosh quietly cried out to the Lord to help her through it.

It was a day of immense joy, because the two young Christians were starting out their lives together with God's blessing. Takoosh was thankful that her daughter had been given a godly husband, but for her, the day felt empty and bleak without Haik there to celebrate with them.

## A MATTER OF LIFE AND DEATH

Takoosh wasn't the only grieving Christian widow in Iran. In December 1990, Pastor Soodmand, a convert from Islam, was hanged near the city of Mashad. His wife, who was blind, had a very hard time coping with his death, but Takoosh was able to share with her what she was going through. Although Mrs. Soodmand was comforted to know that others, like Takoosh, have experienced grief much like her own, she continues to need our prayers.

As it turned out, Haik was not the only Christian pastor to lay down his life in Iran that year. In June, after six months of freedom, Mehdi Dibaj was murdered in a park, leaving his four children behind. He died as a martyr, too, even though the government blamed a terrorist group, the *Moedjaheddin Khalq,* for his sudden death.

Dibaj's body was released only two hours before his funeral, and even then the family was not allowed to open the coffin. This heroic servant of God had been willing to lay down his life from the start. His wife had left him during the years of his detention, and his four children suffered doubly—first they had lost their "adoptive" father, Haik, and now their own father was gone. But like the Hovsepian children, they followed in their father's footsteps and continued to serve the Lord.

Only a few days after Mehdi Dibaj's death, Pastor Tateos Michaelian was shot and killed, leaving his wife, Juliet, and three grown children. Another leader was gone. Pastor Michaelian had succeeded Haik as chairman of the Council of Protestant Pastors in Iran. Only five months after he took on this responsibility, he paid for it with his life. His wife now lives in California with one of her married daughters.

On September 28, 1996, the worldwide Christian community was shaken again. The body of Pastor Ravanbakhsh Yousefi was found hanging from a tree some twenty miles from his house in Ghaem-Shahr. He had left his home early that day to spend time in prayer and meditation. Still another Christian minister had laid down his life in Iran. And another widow, Akhtar, now faced life alone with her two small children.

The sudden death of her husband devastated Akhtar. Today, like Takoosh, she is walking the long road of sorrow, working through her pain step-by-step. Every day at three o'clock, Takoosh calls Akhtar. More than anyone else, she understands what Akhtar is going through.

Christians around the world often pray for their brothers and sisters in Iran, and well we should. These faithful believers are confronted with one of the most virulent persecutions on earth. But a pastor from that country, who visited the States recently, told us, "You pray for us, but maybe you need our prayers more. We cannot afford to wander away from Jesus. We need him so much for every small detail of our lives that we *have* to stay close to him. It's a matter of life and death for us."

That matter of life and death—faith in the Lord Jesus Christ—has been tried and tested in the hearts of Takoosh and her children. They continue to value our prayers for healing, wisdom, and guidance. They live in California now, but dealing with the past and moving courageously into the future continues to challenge them.

But one thing will never change. What Paul wrote to the Christians in Philippi he would surely say to the Hovsepian family and all the other wives and children who have lost their loved ones in Iran: "He who began a good work in you will carry it on to completion until the day of Christ Jesus" (Philippians 1:6).

# NAHED METWALLI

## WHATEVER THE COST

In the bustling city of Cairo, sleek black Mercedes Benz automobiles navigate narrow roadways alongside heavily laden donkey carts. It is a colorful, historic tourist destination, offering an intoxicating array of sights, sounds, and smells. In the shadow of the ancient pyramids, Cairo's population is exploding.

CHAPTER

The kingdom of heaven is like a merchant looking for fine pearls. When he found one of great value, he went away and sold everything he had and bought it.

*Matthew 13:45-46*

But the realities of daily life in Egypt's capital city aren't likely to be found in any travel documentary. There, in one of the world's oldest nations, religious tensions are an everyday reality. For Christians who have converted from Islam, Egypt can be a place of clear and present danger.

Nahed Metwalli was born into a well-to-do Egyptian family, and her relatives held prestigious jobs. Hardworking and ambitious, she became, at an early age, the dean of students at the largest high school for girls in Cairo, achieving that post about ten years ahead of her seniority status. Well-educated, tough-minded and efficient, Nahed was not a woman to be trifled with.

Although she and her husband were estranged, they and their children lived under the same roof. And they lived well. Nahed also had an apartment in the city (quite an accomplishment in a country where engaged couples have to wait four to five years for their own place to live), and she had her own car. Her three children, all in their twenties, seemed to have found their places in life—her son as an engineer, one of her daughters as a secretary, and the other as a teacher.

# PROBLEMS WITH CHRISTIANS

For years Nahed was a devout Muslim who loved and feared her god. And she hated Christians. They did not love the god that she loved. They did not worship him the way she did. Because of this she did everything imaginable to create problems for any Christians who crossed her path, especially the students and teachers with whom she had daily contact. They, in turn, were very much afraid of her.

During the 1986–1987 scholastic year, a Christian principal was appointed to Nahed's school. Nahed could not tolerate the idea of having a Christian boss, so she set about to make the woman's life miserable. Before long, she succeeded in bringing false accusations against the principal, leaving the principal no option but to ask for a transfer to another school. As usual, Nahed won.

Nahed had a restless, dissatisfied spirit, and she seemed to cause trouble wherever she went. After Nahed created a dispute with her secretary, who was a Muslim, the school hired Mary, a Christian, as her replacement. From the beginning she made a good impression on Nahed. Somehow Mary was undaunted by her boss's nasty remarks and unfriendly behavior. And for some strange reason, Nahed actually began to like her.

One day Nahed called Mary into her office. "Do you believe in God?" Nahed asked her.

"There is no God but God," Mary replied with a warm smile.

Nahed could not believe her ears. She had always been told that Christians believe in three gods and worship the Virgin Mary. But her secretary insisted that she was *not* a polytheist. After the two women talked for a while, Mary left the office and left Nahed feeling very disturbed.

During the following weeks Nahed mercilessly tested Mary's honesty, her integrity, and her patience. She shouted at her. She contradicted her own instructions. She tried to trick her into lying. But no matter what was done, Mary remained cheerful. Meanwhile, Nahed grew increasingly anxious.

One night Nahed went to bed feeling very confused. Since she and her husband had decided to remain in the same house for their childrens' sake, she had shared a bedroom with her two daughters. That night sleep would not come. Unresolved religious questions pricked her conscience, keeping her awake and alert. What *was* the truth? Who had the *right* answers about God? Nahed honestly didn't know what to believe anymore.

Finally she prayed: "Please, God, if Christianity is the way to you, show me the Cross. If Islam is the way to you, give me a sign."

## "Is It Over?"

Nahed did not fall asleep. Instead, she found her questions answered in the most extraordinary way.

Never before in her life had she experienced a vision. But now, suddenly, she saw herself standing in a luxurious palace. She could see that she was wearing a long silver robe, and directly in front of her was an empty throne. Elders all dressed in white, with crowns upon their heads, surrounded it.

Suddenly someone entered the palace, and with one voice everyone began to worship him. Nahed followed him with her eyes as he made his way to the throne and seated himself there.

His face was lovely; his eyes were brighter than the sun. Nahed sank to the floor, sitting motionless at his feet. Inside, she was trembling with fear, but despite her terror, she couldn't take her eyes off him. With all her heart she wanted to love him and worship him. A deep peace embraced her.

All at once he spoke. "Is it over, Nahed?"

How did he know her name? She was much too afraid to ask any questions.

"Yes . . . it is over," she replied, barely able to form the words.

She gathered her strength and took another quick look at him, trying to compose herself.

"Are you sure, Nahed?" he asked.

"Yes, I'm sure," she answered.

With the same calm voice he said, "Then I don't have to worry about this matter anymore?"

"No, don't worry about it," she assured him. "It's over."

"Don't be afraid, Nahed. Just look at me."

No words could describe what she saw. Such love, such splendor, such brightness . . .

When the vision ended, Nahed was deeply troubled. She felt weak and shaken. Awakening her family, she pleaded with them to help her understand what she had just seen. Her children and her husband all came up with different answers, none of which satisfied her.

Over the next two or three days, she asked the Christians she knew at school what they thought about the vision. "What was he?" she persistently inquired.

Mary, her secretary, wasn't so sure at all. But she showed Nahed some pictures. One of them, which portrayed Christ, looked somewhat like the man she had seen. But the man in her vision had been far more glorious.

Finally Nahed described her experience to a Christian teacher at her school. He leaned back in his chair, smiled broadly, and exclaimed, "Thank you, Lord! Do you really want to know who he was, Nahed? He was Jesus!"

It wasn't as if she hadn't already known. But at last Nahed was convinced. She broke down and wept for a very long time.

Afterwards, Mary arranged a secret meeting for Nahed with a priest. Mary also knew how to get a Bible. But where would it be safe for Nahed to read it? Certainly not at home with her husband and children around. Her busy office at school, where people kept walking in and out, was not a suitable place either.

Then she remembered her apartment. She had been able to lease it with some of the money she had inherited after her father's death. Suddenly she realized this was God's provision for her. She'd been estranged from her husband for years, and by then her children were in their twenties, and they did not object. So she moved out of the family house and began a new life as a Christian believer.

Now she was able to attend church early in the morning, celebrate mass unnoticed, and continue to meet with the priest for further instruction in her newfound faith. She began to grow in grace as God did his transformative work in her heart.

At school things went on as usual for about a year. But it was obvious to everyone that Nahed had changed. The old, controlling, haughty, and conceited dean they had feared in the past was gone.[4] One day one of her colleagues asked, "Where's the Nahed we used to know?"

Nahed longed to say, "The Nahed you knew is dead, and the Nahed in front of you now is a daughter of Christ!"

Instead, she simply smiled and said, "Now I know God much better, and that's why I've changed. Let bygones be bygones. I want to live a new life."

God continued to speak to Nahed through visions, pictures, and dreams. It was his way of teaching her and showing her what lay ahead. At the beginning of 1989, God impressed upon her heart that Jesus had suffered for her on the cross. As she meditated upon that, she realized that one day she might be called upon to suffer for him. Her thoughts went back to the many trials she had already faced. She had been sick many times. Hardly a year had gone by without an accident or an operation. Could it be that God had saved her life for a special purpose?

## A PERILOUS EXISTENCE

In a country like Egypt, where fundamentalists seek to impose their radical form of Islam upon the population, overt Christian devotion can be perilous. Over a period of weeks, Nahed became aware that the concierge at her apartment building was watching her every move. The more obvious his surveillance became, the more Nahed understood that she would have to find another place to live. But where could she go? To say that the housing shortage in Cairo was severe would have been an understatement.

In June of 1989 Nahed went with some friends to visit a monastery. Some of the monks, impressed by her story, asked her to record her encounter with Christ on tape so that others could be blessed by her testimony. Nahed realized this could be risky, and she prayed about it urgently. But everyone assured her that the tape would be kept very confidential and would never leave the monastery. So she complied with the request.

When Nahed returned to school after summer vacation, she

---

[4] Nahed tells her story in her book *My Encounter with Christ,* published by "The Pen vs. the Sword," P.O. Box 661376, Los Angeles, CA 90066.

immediately sensed that something was wrong. People were cold and rude. Even her Christian friends seemed to be keeping their distance.

"What is going on?" she asked Mary.

At first Mary seemed afraid to talk to her. But she finally called her aside into a private corner. "It's because of the tape," Mary whispered.

"What tape? What are you talking about?"

"The tape where you talk about the vision you had. You know, the one you made at the monastery."

Nahed was horrified. The tape she had recorded with the monks had been duplicated and distributed throughout the community. To make matters worse, she had mentioned several names of Christian colleagues on the recording. So now the Muslims knew.

What God revealed to her in private was now known in public. She never learned which of the monks had betrayed her trust, or why, but within twenty days the tape found its way around the whole country. Nahed had no choice but to resign her school position. And she had to find another apartment, too. But where?

With the help of Christian friends, she started moving from one place to another. One day one of her Christian friends took her for a walk in a remote area. "I need to talk to you, Nahed."

"Why? What's wrong?"

"I just learned that Father Zakaria has been arrested," the friend explained. "And we think it has something to do with you."

"Oh, God, forgive me! What will happen to him?"

"I don't know. But he's not the only one. Mary is having some problems, too."

"What do you mean?"

"She's been fired, and it looks like the police may be watching her."

Nahed was stunned and frightened. By now she was living her life on the run, always looking over her shoulder.

The next day, as she knelt in her church, a fellow parishioner slipped into the pew beside her and pretended to be praying aloud.

"A policeman is in the back, talking to the priest about you," he murmured. "I think he wants to ask you some questions."

"What shall I do?" Nahed's stared straight ahead, her heart racing. "Where shall I go?"

"Behind the altar is a back door. Go forward, and slip around the side to the back. Go now. God be with you, sister!"

Without a backward glance, Nahed moved to the front, knelt briefly before the altar, then slowly moved to her right and made her way out the back door.

She barely escaped.

Back at the house where she had been staying, one of her daughters telephoned. "Mom, the police were here looking for you. I told them you were away on holiday. Are you all right?"

Nahed knew very well that her days in Egypt were numbered. She had become a liability to everyone she knew, especially to those who were trying to help. Her family was putting immense pressure on her to return to Islam, and it was obvious that they would not hesitate to take drastic measures.

*God, what am I to do?* she prayed, unsure of her next move.

## New Country, New Life

Nahed did receive help. The Lord undertook, and after a series of narrow escapes, Nahed was miraculously able to flee Egypt and settle in Holland. Thankfully her daughter, who also had found Christ, went with her.

Once Johan and I learned about Nahed's situation and that she was in our country, we were able to visit her on several occasions. The first time we visited, she and her daughter were still in hiding. They had not yet received refugee status and were living under assumed names.

Johan and I scoured a map, trying to find our way to the small, obscure village where Nahed and her daughter had been provided with an apartment. As we drove along a winding countryside road trying to find the place, Johan chuckled, "At least they'll be safe. No

Egyptian secret policeman on earth is going to find them all the way out here!"

Our hearts were moved when we saw the way the two women, who had once enjoyed affluence, now were living. Their room contained only the most basic furniture. On the walls hung a few pictures of saints who are revered in the Coptic Church. Otherwise, Nahed and her daughter had lost everything. Isolated in this rural area in a foreign country, they were separated from their loved ones. It was a challenge for them to communicate—the Dutch language is not easy to master. And how bored they must have been with no job to go to every day and with no familiar television programs or other diversions. Local Christians were making every effort to minister to them. But they had to be careful—Nahed was not out of danger yet.

Gradually the situation improved. The next time we met, Nahed had moved to the city of Leiden. "Please call me Nahed now," she asked. "I want to be called by my real name now that I have refugee status!"

She enthusiastically told us about the Coptic Church in Amsterdam she now was attending. "And I've even found an Egyptian friend nearby," she said with a smile.

But Nahed shared with me a burden that was on her heart. "Back in Egypt," she confided, "shortly after my conversion, the Lord spoke to me through Acts 26:16, "I have appeared to you to appoint you as a servant and as a witness of what you have seen of me and what I will show you." At the time I wondered what he meant by that. Was he talking about the cassette tapes of my testimony, or did he have some other ministry for me?"

"What do you think now? Has he told you anything else?"

"I prayed about it for a long time, and now I think I've heard His voice in my heart. *No, this is not the end of your ministry,* he seems to be saying. *You didn't understand what I meant when I said to you in the vision 'Don't be afraid, just look at me.' You are still afraid, Nahed. You look to human beings. Again I say to you, 'Don't be afraid. Stand up. You will be my servant and my witness.'*"

"What does he want you to do, Nahed?"

She shook her head uncertainly. "I know that he wants to use me, but where? and when?"

## THE PEARL OF GREAT PRICE

Johan and I had no easy answers for her, but we assured her that God would open up the right doors for her when he felt it was time. "For now," Johan told her, "all you can do is be faithful where the Lord has placed you. Be faithful in your church, with the people in your neighborhood, with the others who share your house. God always wants us to first minister to the people around us."

Not long after our visit Nahed called. "Anneke, guess what? I've been invited to speak in America!"

Her travel documents were issued, and she left on a speaking tour to several Egyptian churches in the United States. Later, she was featured in a documentary on Dutch television aimed at reaching Holland's Muslims with the gospel.

I was delighted with her good news. "So, you're beginning to get some answers?" I asked.

"Yes, at last!"

"Do you hear from your family, Nahed?" I asked. Her family was now aware that she was living in the Netherlands.

"Yes," she answered quietly. "Not long ago my son called me. He tried to convince me to return to Egypt. He told me that if I would become a Muslim again, everything would be forgiven and forgotten. I've brought shame on the family name, and they are obliged to do what they can to make me return to Islam. I understand that. But it was very difficult for me to hear my son say that he loved me and that he longed for me to come home!"

Nahed's voice broke with emotion. I could imagine the temptation to return had been very real. Nahed deeply loved her children, and living in her native country again must, at times, have seemed very attractive.

Reflecting on my conversations with Nahed, I am reminded of the parable of the pearl of great price. Jim Elliot understood it decades before as he set out to meet the Auca Indians in Ecuador: "He is no fool who gives what he cannot keep to gain what he cannot lose."

That young missionary and four others paid with their lives, but today there is a church among the Auca Indians.

Nahed's life testifies to the same truth. "I will never give up my

Jesus!" she has said repeatedly. Considering what she has been through, her words never fail to touch me deeply.

Last time I talked to her, I quietly whispered a prayer after we said good-bye. "Lord, help me to be true to you—whatever the cost. And please help Nahed fulfill your purpose for her life. That's really all she wants, Lord. In fact, it's all she has left."

# SARAH

## FOR BETTER OR FOR WORSE

Dressed in her nurse's uniform, "Sarah" made her way through her familiar hospital rounds, struggling to concentrate. She looked in on one patient after another, checking vital signs, offering encouragement, and trying to keep herself focused.

CHAPTER

Your Father, who sees
what is done in secret,
will reward you.

*Matthew 6:18*

As she walked into a ward where an elderly woman was recovering from an operation, the woman's plaintive appeal jarred her, "Nurse, I'm hurting so much; the pain is killing me. Please—give me another shot!"

Sarah could immediately see that the old woman was really suffering. She'd had abdominal surgery the afternoon before, and her postoperative pain was at its worst. Sarah carefully took her pulse and blood pressure and checked the chart—four hours since the last injection. "You're right, it's time for more medication," she told the woman. "I'll be right back."

Hurriedly, Sarah prepared a syringe. *I'm so glad she can have another shot,* she thought. *She's really hurting, and in a few more minutes she'll be sleeping pain-free. If only there were some kind of medicine that would take care of the pain in my own heart. . . .*

That particular morning Sarah was aching with worry.

Only a few hours before she had taken her two young children to a friend's house for day care. She had then boarded a minibus to go to work. It was her standard routine, but today something had happened that made her feel very uneasy.

As she walked along the dusty road with her two children, a man walked behind them. She had no idea who he was, but she vaguely recognized his face. Wasn't he the same man she'd seen the day before, standing across the street when she came home? Come to think of it, he often seemed to be around when she was taking the children to their baby-sitter. Sarah was fairly sure she had also seen him in the minibus on her way to the hospital.

Suddenly, it occurred to Sarah that the man might not be there by accident. What if he was following her? What if he was trying to find out where she was taking the children?

The more Sarah thought about the incident, the more concerned she became. She knew that the only way her husband's family could hurt her husband now was by kidnapping his children. What else would give Hassan a reason to come home?

## FORBIDDEN FAITH

"This will get you through the worst of it," Sarah said. "By this afternoon it won't be so bad." She gave the woman her injection, made note of it on the chart, and smoothed the bedding.

As she worked, Sarah remembered . . .

Sarah had met Hassan at a friend's house seven years ago. Since in their culture it was not proper for a man and woman to be alone unless they were related or married, she had gotten to know him sipping countless cups of tea in the homes of various friends. Oblivious to the people around them, Hassan and Sarah spent hours talking. That's how she learned about his past ordeals.

Although he was raised in a Muslim family, Islam never meant much to Hassan. An integral part of the culture in which he grew up, it never met his spiritual or emotional needs. Then one day in 1976 a friend at work told him about Jesus. When the gospel was explained to Hassan, he knew in his heart that this was the truth he had been searching for.

With great joy, Hassan asked God to forgive his sins and invited Jesus into his life. But as soon as he accepted the claims of Christ, his troubles began.

When his family found out that he had become a Christian, they did everything they could to make him renounce his newfound faith. They threatened him. They beat him. On many occasions his body was left bruised and bleeding after their attacks.

"You have brought shame on our family!" Hassan's brother shouted at him one day. "If you think beatings are the only thing you'll have to endure, you're sadly mistaken. We will not stop there. You know very well what Islamic law says—we are to use every possible means to force you to return to Islam. And we will, Hassan, I warn you! If you don't renounce your Christian faith, we won't hesitate to kill you!"

Hassan was startled by the hatred he saw flashing in his brother's eyes. There was no doubt but that he meant what he said. Even so, his brother's threats were easier to bear than his mother's tears.

Whenever they were alone, she begged him to come to his senses and listen to his father and brothers. "I love you, Hassan," she would cry. "I don't want to lose you. Can't you just go to the mosque with them again and pretend you're still a Muslim? I'm so afraid they'll kill you!"

Hassan was a man of principle, and he refused to give in. He knew he had found the truth, and he was determined to live for Jesus, no matter what it cost him. So in 1982, with his life in constant danger and his situation unbearable, Hassan decided to leave the country. For five years he found work and refuge in a series of neighboring countries.

But he was homesick. He missed his friends, and he longed to see his family, especially his mother. Surely it would be safe to return, at least for a brief visit. *Time heals all wounds*, he assured himself as he made his travel arrangements.

## AN UNUSUAL FAMILY REUNION

As soon as his brothers found out that Hassan was back in town, one of them contacted him.

"We're so glad you've come back," he said, smiling. "Mother can't wait to see you. We've come to realize that the way we treated you in the past was wrong, and we want to welcome you back into the family. Can you come for dinner Saturday evening?"

Overjoyed, Hassan accepted the invitation. His prayers had been answered. He couldn't wait to be with his relatives again.

Soon he was in the welcoming arms of his father and brothers. His mother was weeping when she greeted him, but this time she cried tears of joy. It was obvious she had done everything possible to make the reunion a happy occasion. The marble floor was shining. The Persian rugs were neatly vacuumed. The table was overloaded with food. The smell of roast lamb, curried chicken, and several other of his favorite dishes filled the room. Delicate green mint leaves, which decorated most of the dishes, told Hassan that he really was home again.

The atmosphere remained pleasant throughout the evening. As they dipped their fingers into the food, his father and brothers talked about the family business. And in exchange, without giving too much detailed information, Hassan told them a little bit about his travels abroad.

Not a harsh word was spoken. Nobody tried to convince Hassan that Islam was the only way. *Have they finally accepted the fact that I won't recant?* he asked himself.

It wasn't long before he knew the answer.

After thanking his family for a wonderful evening, Hassan decided to stop by a Christian friend's house on the way back to his apartment. While he was there, he suddenly became very sick. His arms and legs prickled and went to sleep, his eyes rolled back into their sockets, and his body convulsed with pain. His friend recognized the symptoms immediately. He knew Hassan had just returned from a meal at his family's house.

"You've been poisoned," he told Hassan grimly, rushing to get him to the hospital. They arrived just in time, and Hassan's stomach was pumped dry. He was sick for days, but he survived the ordeal.

That was the last time he saw his family. Now that his brothers knew where to find him, Hassan had to keep moving. For a while he was a fugitive in his own country.

It was during this time that Sarah met him. She was captivated by the stories he told her about his years abroad. She enjoyed his sense of humor. But she especially admired his dedication to Jesus, the Savior she had known from childhood.

## Love Has Its Price

"Sarah, will you marry me?" Hassan asked her one day. His proposal didn't come as a total surprise. Sarah was aware, as they had become better and better acquainted, that Hassan felt as drawn to her as she did to him. But she also realized that a positive answer could have severe repercussions.

Sarah knew only too well that a Muslim-background believer was never safe in their country. Only very recently the church she had attended from childhood had been vividly reminded of that ugly state of affairs.

Their pastor, who was from a Muslim family, had come to Christ forty years before and had pastored his church for more than twenty years. Just days before, two men on a motorcycle suddenly roared into the church compound, where the pastor happened to be working outside. As the motorcycle pulled up next to him, one man jumped off the bike, flashing a knife, which had been hidden in his shirtsleeve. He tried to stab the pastor and nearly succeeded.

Inside the house, the pastor's family heard him shouting, "Jesus, protect me!" His wife and daughter rushed out in time to see the motorcycle disappearing in a cloud of dust. A gardener had come to the pastor's aid, which had probably scared the assailants away and saved the pastor's life.

Sarah's pastor had been unhurt, but his congregation was left in a state of shock. How could it be that forty years after conversion a Muslim convert's life was still in danger?

With this in mind, Sarah had some serious thinking to do. If she married Hassan, it was quite possible that he would be hiding from his family for the rest of his days. And she would be hiding with him. Was it worth it? Eventually, with her parents' and her pastor's consent, Sarah decided to marry Hassan anyway. The couple's love was stronger than reason.

Sarah would always cherish the memory of her beautiful 1992 wedding day. Of course no one from Hassan's family was present. Only Sarah's family members and her Christian friends were invited. Dressed in her elegant traditional dress and accompanied by her two sisters as bridesmaids, Sarah walked to the front of the church on her father's arm. The smile on her bridegroom's face made it all worthwhile. This was the man she loved, the only man she would ever want to marry.

But Sarah did swallow hard before she repeated the words "For better for worse, for richer for poorer . . ." What did the future hold for them? The only thing she and Hassan were certain about was their love for each other. Would that love prove to be strong enough to get them through the "worse" and the "poorer"?

*God help us,* she prayed silently. *You're the only one who can make a marriage like this work.*

It wasn't long before their troubles began in earnest.

## A FAR-REACHING DECISION

"Sarah, come quickly! Hassan has had an accident!" Layla's pale, worried face spoke volumes about Hassan's condition. Sarah quickly grabbed her scarf, covered her head, and rushed into the waiting taxi. As they raced to the hospital, Layla told Sarah what had happened.

Layla's husband, John, and Hassan worked for the same company. Hassan was a successful salesman. Everyone knew that he did his job well; people liked him, and he made good money. As far as anyone at work knew, he had no enemies.

About an hour before, as Hassan crossed the street in front of the company's headquarters, a car had hit him. Layla's husband, John, arrived on the scene almost immediately. He'd called his wife from the hospital, and she went to get Sarah. At the time they had no idea how badly Hassan was hurt.

The taxi ride seemed to go on forever, and Sarah was nearly frantic with worry. Why were all these animals on the road? She looked out just as a little child shoved her grubby hand through the window, begging for loose change. Sarah turned her face away in annoyance.

"Please, can't you hurry?" she urged the driver.

The driver threw his hands up in exasperation. He simply couldn't go any faster.

Eventually, after what seemed like a lifetime, they arrived at the hospital, where John was pacing and waiting for them. "They've taken him in for surgery," John informed Sarah. "I don't think we need to fear for his life, but his leg is badly hurt. They aren't sure they can save it. All we can do is wait."

"Oh, God, don't let him lose his leg!" Layla prayed aloud.

"Did you see it happen?" Sarah asked, fighting for composure.

"No, I didn't," he told her, "but the commotion on the street attracted my attention, so I went to look outside. There were a couple of witnesses, and they told me the car that overran Hassan came hurtling out of nowhere. They said it almost seemed like it meant to hit him! I guess it was just one of those strange accidents."

Several hours later Sarah was finally able to talk to Hassan. "It was no accident," he told her quietly. "It was intentional."

"Did you see who was driving?" she asked.

"No, all I saw was the car, and it wasn't a car I recognized. But this much I know—it was an attack on my life." His face was ashen with pain, and the worry in his eyes was intense.

"So you think your family knows where you are?" Sarah asked him the question that had been lingering in her mind all day.

"I'm not sure, but I wouldn't doubt it. When you think about it, who else would be trying to kill me?"

Hassan recovered completely, though for a while it seemed that he might lose the use of his leg. But the "accident" was a turning point both for him and for Sarah. From that day on, they knew that it was just a matter of time before Hassan was attacked again.

Still, all things considered, the first few years of their marriage were happy. First, the Lord gave them a little girl. A year later a son was added to the family. Hassan loved his children dearly, and they loved their father. Every day Emily counted the minutes until he came home from work. As soon as she heard the sound of her father's motorcycle, she scurried outside. Hassan would lift her up onto his shoulders, also scooping up little John who had just started to walk, along the way.

Sometimes, when the weather was nice, Hassan took his wife and children to the park for a picnic. The four of them laughed together, and for a few hours at least, even Hassan and Sarah were able to forget about their troubles. The comfort of his wife and children's love helped ease Hassan's loss of his parents and brothers.

As time went by, Hassan grew increasingly concerned about the future. His responsibility for the safety of his wife and children weighed heavily upon him. He knew that his family had not forgotten him. They would continue their search. As far as Hassan was concerned, it would just be a matter of time before disaster struck again.

"Sarah, we need to talk," he said one evening after the children had gone to bed. "I have been thinking that it might be better for us all to leave the country. I don't feel safe at work, and I worry constantly about you and the children. I can't seem to shake off this uneasy feeling that somebody is after me. I think it would be good if we tried to save as much money as we can. Once we've set enough aside, we can just quietly go."

"But Hassan, I'd miss my family too much. And what about my job at the hospital?" Sarah protested. "Do you really think the situation is that bad? Let's just think about it for a while. Besides, how are you going to get the necessary papers to leave the country? You can't tell the truth about your reason for going. So what will you do?"

"Don't worry about that," Hassan assured Sarah. "My friend Stephen has a friend in the government. He knows people who may be willing to help us. Not every Muslim hates Christians—you know that. Some of them are as upset as we are about the way we've been treated. Look, why don't we just pray together and ask the Lord to lead us?"

Hassan took Sarah's hand and began to pray. It helped to calm her down. But she continued to have very mixed emotions about leaving her country and her family.

Meanwhile, at least superficially, life continued as usual. Hassan worked as hard as ever, but he began to invest every bit of extra money he earned in jewelry. He bought an iron safe with a solid lock and hid all the money he could afford to lay aside, as well as the jewelry, inside.

In the meantime his friend Stephen did what he could to get the paperwork ready for the family to leave the country. It seemed best that Hassan should go first. Sarah would follow later with the children.

"It will look suspicious if we try to process papers for everyone at once," Stephen had explained to Hassan. "This way it just looks like you're going on a business trip abroad."

Sarah hated the thought of being left alone with the children. But as time went by, and she and Hassan continued to pray about the plan together, she agreed to her husband's proposal. The thought of Hassan's death was more frightening to her than anything else she could imagine.

Just days before his departure, Sarah made a shocking discovery.

"Hassan, come here, quickly!" she shouted from the basement. From the sound of her voice, her husband knew something was terribly wrong.

Sarah had gone down early in the morning to remove some clothes from storage. As she made her way down the stairs, she immediately noticed the disorder. The door to one of their closets had been forcefully opened. Clothes and papers littered the floor. And in the middle of the mess lay their steel safe, which Hassan had stuck away in the corner of a cupboard. Hidden from prying eyes, it had contained all the jewelry and money they had saved. It was to have been the beginning of their new life in some future country of refuge.

Rushing down to the basement Hassan immediately realized what had happened. Burglars had forcefully opened the safe with a steel bar. Everything he had worked for was gone.

Hassan and Sarah sat staring at each other in disbelief. What could they do? Calling the police would be absurd. How could they explain why they had so much money in the house? Hassan couldn't very well tell the authorities the reason for his savings. Besides, thieves were rarely caught.

A thought nagged at them. How did the thieves know about the money? Who would have guessed that they'd stashed so much money in the house? They didn't look like rich people. Could one of their acquaintances have been involved in this robbery?

"We're more vulnerable than ever," Hassan told his wife sadly. "There's no end to this."

Hassan and Sarah never found out who stole their money and jewelry. But Hassan decided to leave the country anyway. Friends had promised to help him find a job when he arrived in his country of refuge, so he and Sarah agreed that Hassan should leave as soon as possible. Then Stephen could start working on the papers for Sarah and the children to join him.

## A Painful Separation

It was agonizingly difficult for Hassan to leave Sarah, and she felt ripped apart by his departure. She was glad the children were too small to realize fully what was happening. When he left, they thought their father was just kissing them good-bye and going to work. But as time went by, they began asking more and more frequently for Daddy to come home. Their sad questions intensified the longing in Sarah's own heart.

To get the necessary papers for her and the children took much longer than anyone anticipated. First there was the month of Ramadan. It seemed like everybody's mind was on something other than work during that holy month. Then once Ramadan was over, other obstacles surfaced. Weeks turned into months, and little progress was made.

Hassan called regularly, and that helped ease Sarah's mind. "I miss you and the children terribly," he told her every time he called. "I hope and pray it won't be long until you're here with me."

Sarah could hardly wait. Gone was her reluctance to leave. And now, with this new fear that she was being followed and that her children might be kidnapped, their departure seemed like a matter of life and death.

*Oh, Lord, please, protect them!* she prayed as she continued to commute to work and await her husband's next telephone call. *Keep them safe, and help Stephen find a way to get us out of here!*

One evening Sarah's phone rang. "Sarah, it's me—Layla," her friend began. "Look, a visitor from abroad would like to see you. If you want, John will pick you up from the hospital tomorrow afternoon and take you to the place where she's staying. Don't worry about the kids. I'll look after them until you get home."

Sarah was puzzled. Who would want to come and see her? She had never been abroad and didn't know any foreigners. *I wonder if Hassan has anything to do with this?* she asked herself.

That very evening her husband called. "I am going to see a special visitor," she told him. " Do you know who it might be?"

Hassan couldn't say too much on the phone, but he knew exactly who and what she meant. He breathed a prayer of thanks that the connection had been made.

## A Precious Gift

I was the visitor who went to see Sarah.

On a trip to the Middle East, Johan and I were introduced to Hassan. When he told us his story, we were deeply touched. We'd always known that there are many Muslim-background believers like Hassan and Sarah in the Muslim world and that the price they pay for following Jesus is indescribable. We had come face-to-face with one of them.

"Where does your wife live?" I asked when Hassan finished talking. To my surprise and delight, he named the city that was the next stop on our trip.

"Would it cause her any trouble to see me?" I asked. "Could I meet with her?"

"Sure, you can," he said. "We'll just arrange for her to come to your hotel."

With the help of friends, only a few days later I found myself sitting with Sarah in a Middle Eastern hotel room. She was still dressed in her white hospital uniform.

Before our trip, I knew nothing about Sarah or her ordeal. I had never heard of Hassan or his dangerous background. But God knew all about them, and before we left home, he had encouraged me to take along a special gift.

Years ago at an Open Doors USA prayer conference, an elderly woman had asked to talk to me. "The Lord told me to give you this," she explained, pressing a small box in my hand. "Use it however you wish."

When I opened it, I found a beautiful ring. *This is for the Suffering Church,* I told myself. *I'll sell it and then take the money to Vietnam.* We were scheduled to fly to Saigon the next month.

I had no idea how much the ring was worth, so I had it appraised by a jeweler friend. She told me the ring was made of gold, and the cluster contained numerous small diamonds. She appraised it at $2,000. When I tried to sell it, though, I couldn't get more than $216. So I stored the ring away in a drawer, and there it stayed for more than five years, waiting for better economic times.

Now as I left on this trip, I felt compelled to take the ring along.

Through Christine Mallouhi's book *Mini-skirts, Mothers and Muslims,*[5] I had learned the importance of jewelry in Muslim culture. It is a way husbands show appreciation for their wives. Over the years I had noticed that women in some poor countries sometimes wear surprisingly beautiful jewelry. I now understood that it demonstrated their value as women.

So I had brought the ring along on this trip, not really understanding why. When Hassan told us about their jewelry being stolen, I knew exactly who it was for.

"Sarah," I said after we'd talked for a while, "I have a gift for you." I took the small, neatly wrapped jewelry box out of my purse.

"The same year you married Hassan, someone gave me this ring. God knew that one day in the future, you would need encouragement. The ring is for you, to let you know that God knows all about your situation. He cares for you, Sarah. You are very precious in his sight."

As Sarah opened the box, her eyes brimmed with tears. It wasn't the first time that afternoon that we'd been crying.

As a mother, I empathized with Sarah when she shared her concern for her children. As a wife, I could understand how painfully she missed her husband. Now Sarah's tears were tears of joy and gratitude, because she realized that God loved her and remembered her. Her future and that of her family were in his good hands.

"You can do with the ring whatever you like," I said. "If you want to sell it, that's fine with me. If you prefer to keep it, that's okay too."

It was hard for me to say good-bye to Sarah. I would soon be leaving her country, while she would have to stay—at least for the time being. Nobody could tell for sure when she would be able to join her husband.

That special afternoon God showed all of us that he has not forgotten his suffering children in the Muslim world.

Sarah kept the ring. "I am never going to sell this," she told a friend later on. "For me, it's a symbol of God's loving care. Every time I look at it, I remember him. This ring is a constant reminder that he hasn't forgotten me."

---

[5]Christine Mallouhi, *Mini-skirts, Mothers and Muslims* (Carlisle, UK: Spear Publications, 1994).

# IMM BASEM

## NO EASY SOLUTIONS

Soldiers. Soldiers. Soldiers everywhere. Soldiers entered our bus for a security check when we crossed the River Jordan, driving into Israel from Jordan. Soldiers watched closely as we came out of the bus terminal. Soldiers guarded the lookout point on the Mount of Olives, which we passed on the way to Bethlehem. This was the Holy Land, where political instability rules and peace can never be counted on for long.

CHAPTER

"I know the plans I have for you," declares the Lord, "plans to prosper you and not to harm you, plans to give you hope and a future."

*Jeremiah 29:11*

Johan and I were on our way to Bethlehem Bible College, our last stop on a two-week trip to three Middle Eastern countries. We disembarked our bus, made our way to the school, and located the office of Alex Awad, the college's vice principal. Alex jumped to his feet to greet us as we walked in.

"Welcome, welcome! It's so good to see you!" Alex's smile was as warm as his handshake. After visiting friends in Lebanon and Jordan, we were growing very fond of the generous Middle Eastern hospitality. There's really nothing like it in the world.

After we settled down in his office, Alex said, "Now please let me know what you'd like to see while you are here." His words reminded me that we hadn't yet explored Israel or Jerusalem. "We have trained tour guides here at the college who be would more than willing to take you around."

Johan smiled. "Well, we know that a lot of people come to see the ancient landmarks, but we've come to see what the Bible calls 'living stones,'" he explained. "We'd like to meet some real people and hear what life is like for them on the West Bank."

Brother Andrew had told us a lot about the suffering of the Palestinian people. I soon found out that Bethlehem College is far more than a Bible school. It is also a place of refuge, help, and hope for many people in the surrounding towns and refugee camps.

## AN UNEXPLAINABLE INTRUSION

During the following days, Alex himself functioned as our guide. One afternoon we found ourselves in a community called Beit Jala, one of the three predominantly Christian towns on the West Bank. There Alex introduced us to Imm and Abu Basem. "They have quite a story to tell you," he said, smiling.

As we looked around the house, we noticed its spaciousness and grace. It was far more comfortable than the Muslim home we'd visited the day before. Most Palestinian people who lived in Israel had their homes taken from them in 1948. The United Nations provided cement cubicles in camps on the West Bank for Palestinian refugees who fled to Jordan after Israel became an independent state. Abu Basem's home, however, had been in the family for generations. Because the West Bank was part of Jordan at the time, this family was able to stay in their house. But like many of the refugees we visited, they, too, had borne their share of suffering.

"When I heard you were coming, I took a sedative," Imm Basem confided with a nervous laugh. "Last Sunday night I told my story at a *Musalaha* (reconciliation) meeting for Jewish and Palestinian Christian ladies. I got so emotional in the end that I couldn't finish. One of my friends had to help me. You know, after all these years, it still hurts when I think of what happened to my son."

Johan and I glanced at each other. "We want very much to hear about your son's situation," I said. "But please don't feel nervous."

Imm nodded, took a deep breath, and began. "On February 5, 1989, in the middle of the night, soldiers from the Israeli secret police came to our house. They asked for our son Khadar, who was a student at Bethlehem Bible College at the time. He was not at home—he'd been invited to spend that night at the college.

"The Israeli police ordered my husband to go and get him. In the meantime no less than forty-two soldiers flooded our house.

They began searching through our possessions, ransacking the drawers and cupboards, and turning everything upside down. The girls started crying. . . ."

Soldiers aimed their flashlights at Imm's daughters. They stroked the girls' hair. "We just want to make sure they're girls," one of them explained with a sly smile.

The two sisters, already frightened by the unexpected intrusion, began to scream.

"Please!" Imm pleaded with the soldiers. "Leave my girls and our furniture alone! I'll answer all your questions; we have nothing to hide. But what do you need Khadar for? Basem is our oldest son. Don't you want him?"

The family was not politically active, and Imm couldn't imagine why the Israeli soldiers had come in the first place. She pleaded with them until her husband arrived with Khadar. Then they all watched in stunned silence as the soldiers roughly blindfolded Khadar and drove away with him into the snowy February night.

At first Imm and her husband were advised to simply wait and pray. "He hasn't done anything wrong, and they'll soon realize that," one of the school administrators told them. But seventeen days passed with no word, no explanation—nothing. At last, Imm could no longer bear the uncertainty.

She made her way to the Israeli police station and went inside. "I need to see my son," she told the officer in charge.

"That's not possible," the unsmiling officer snapped. "He's in solitary confinement. He is not being cooperative and is unwilling to confess. You aren't going to see him until he confesses."

"Confesses to what?" Imm inquired as patiently as possible.

The officer shook his head, as if to say the conversation was over. He gestured for Imm to get out.

## An Unlikely Friend

After twenty-two days, the family was informed that a lawyer could visit Khadar. With the help of the college administrators, a lawyer was found. Imm hurriedly prepared a parcel for her son, containing some clean underwear and his Bible. She sent it along with the lawyer.

Khadar and the lawyer talked quietly for a few minutes, and the young man received his mother's parcel with great appreciation. But once the lawyer left, the soldiers standing guard around Khadar grabbed the Bible and the clean clothes and roughly shoved him back into his cell. "Once you decide to confess," one of them laughed, holding the underwear up for all to see, "maybe you can have these back."

Khadar had resolutely kept his emotions in check up until that moment. Now he collapsed on his bed and wept bitterly. The hours crawled by, and he lay on his cot silent and motionless, in absolute despair. He wanted to pray, but the only thought he could summon from the depths of his heart was, *God help me. . . .*

Later that night he heard a knock on his cell door. A voice quietly called him to the window. A young Israeli soldier was standing there, holding a Bible in his hand.

"Is this your Bible?" the soldier asked.

"Yes."

"Are you a believer?" the stranger whispered.

"Yes, I am," Khadar answered, bewildered by the question.

"So am I. Here—take your Bible and hide it."

Before Khadar could ask his name, the soldier disappeared into the darkness. Deeply moved, the young Palestinian man held the Bible close to his heart and wept. Why had the soldier given it to him? Was it some kind of a trick? Or was it an answer to his desperate prayer?

The same soldier returned to Khadar's cell on several other occasions. One day he brought a meat sandwich, which Khadar was afraid to eat. He wanted to trust his anonymous friend, but how could he be sure that the sandwich wasn't poisoned? Understanding the young prisoner's hesitation, the Israeli soldier took a small bite out of the sandwich himself to prove it was safe. Another time he brought Khadar a bottle of water to drink. Again, although he was very thirsty, the prisoner was afraid to drink. Without a word, the soldier took a sip first.

After gratefully drinking the water, Khadar asked God for a sign. "Lord, if that soldier really wants to help me, let him bring me a piece of Elite chocolate."

Later that same day there was another knock on his cell-block door. "I'm sorry, Khadar," the soldier said, "I couldn't get you any bread, but you have to keep your strength up. Eat this, instead."

From his pocket he took a piece of Elite chocolate.

"Why are you helping me?" Khadar asked his new friend.

"Because you're my brother, through the blood of Christ. And I don't want you to be in here."

The soldier did more than minister to Khadar; he went home and told his father about the suffering of his Palestinian friend. The father knew Bishara Awad, the president of Bethlehem Bible College, and called him. And that's how Imm and Abu Basem learned that Khadar was still alive.

Khadar spent a total of fifty-two days in solitary confinement in a cell not big enough for him to stand up in. There were many days when he was given nothing to eat or drink. He was interrogated daily and, on more than one occasion, tortured. Never once was he allowed to wash himself or to change his underwear.

## FINDING THE WAY HOME

As Imm Basem came to this part of her story, she began to struggle with her emotions. More and more often, she had to stop and wipe tears from her eyes. I tried to imagine how I would feel if something like that had happened to one of my sons. It was unthinkable.

"Finally, Khadar was released," Imm continued. "An Israeli Army captain came to his cell and told him he was being taken to a prison in the desert. My son picked up his Bible, which had the wrapping paper from the piece of chocolate inside it, and followed the captain. When they got to the door, the officer turned to Khadar and said, "Run! Go home to your family!"

Khadar was released without being charged, tried, or fined. He never confessed to anything because he had nothing to confess.[6]

---

[6]Khadar's story is told by Lynn Weaver in *Who from Our Mother's Arms* (Bristol, UK: Friendly Press). ISBN 0-948728-24-8. Friendly Press, 300 Gloucester Road, Bristol BS7 8PD, UK

Relieved that she had made it this far into the story, Imm stopped for a moment to have a sip of the soda her daughter had brought to us. She wiped her eyes and stood up to stretch herself before continuing.

Her husband, Abu, picked up the story at that point. "At first Khadar had no idea where he was. He had been blindfolded when they took him to prison, and now it was dark. He walked around aimlessly and finally came to some houses. After knocking on several doors, a Muslim family took him in."

"I wish I knew that family," Imm Basem interrupted. "They were so good to my son, and I want to thank them. I've tried to find them, but I don't know where they live."

The kindhearted Muslim people gave Khadar a small meal and invited him to sleep on their couch until morning. Then they took him to the bus and gave him money for the fare home. On Hebron Road, which goes right through Bethlehem to Beit Jala, he tried to get a lift, but nobody recognized him. Sick and thin, he bore little resemblance to the man who had been arrested weeks before. Worst of all, he smelled terrible—everyone in the room well remembered the horrible stench Khadar had brought into the house.

Imm Basem began to weep as she recalled that bittersweet reunion. The memory of seeing her son in such a pitiful state still breaks her heart. But her eyes lit up when we asked her how Khadar was doing now.

"Khadar recovered physically and emotionally," she said, drawing a shaky breath. "He went on to graduate from Bethlehem Bible College, and he received a scholarship to study in Cairo, where he earned his B.A."

She went on to tell us that Khadar had fallen in love with a Palestinian nurse from the United States while she visited the West Bank. They got married, and Khadar continued his studies in America. He was then pastoring a church in the States and was about to receive his M.A.

"So life has worked out all right for him, in spite of everything?" I ventured.

"Perhaps, but I wish it were the same for our other children," Imm Basem said, shaking her head sadly. "You know, even though the *intifada* (Palestinian uprising) is over now, we are still suffering.

We are not free. Did you notice the roadblock when you entered the West Bank? Often the Israelis close the road entirely. We need permission every time we want to go past that roadblock."

## REASONS FOR HOPE

As she finished talking to us, Imm said the saddest words I heard during our time on the West Bank. "We know how to say the word *peace;* we know how to write it, but we do not know what it means. There is no future here for us and for our children."

Was she right? Is there no future for the Palestinian people on the West Bank? I wasn't quite prepared to agree with her, because Johan and I had seen and heard a few signs of hope during our trip.

Imm Basem herself told us that they had received a phone call from the soldier who had helped their son. "Would you allow a Jewish soldier to come to your house?" he asked.

"Yes, of course!" they answered. "But please come in your civilian clothes," they added cautiously.

The soldier arrived literally trembling with fear. Visiting a Palestinian home was not an everyday occurrence for a Jewish soldier. "I'm scared," he admitted. "For years I believed what I was told, that all Palestinians are bad people—that all of you are stone-throwers and killers. Now I know that is not true."

That first time he stayed for two and a half hours, but many more visits followed. When he announced his engagement, the Basem family attended the betrothal ceremony. When he was married, they went to the wedding. They became friends for life. Their common love for Jesus the Messiah was stronger than their political differences.

Traveling with a friend to Gaza, we heard stories of Muslims coming to Christ, even in that dirty, despondent place. Missionaries have faithfully worked in Gaza for over thirteen years. A Christian bookstore was recently opened there, a joint project of the Bible Society and Open Doors. On the West Bank there was also a Christian presence, comprised of both missionaries and national Christians faithfully fulfilling their God-given mission.

Perhaps the most encouraging development was *Musalaha.*

Salim Munayer, a Palestinian, started this movement several years ago. It was his vision to bring Jewish and Palestinian Christians together to share about their hurts, to listen to each other, and to bring into practice Jesus' admonition to love our enemies.[7] It has been a slow and painful process, but it is beginning to bear fruit.

Imm Basem herself is part of *Musalaha*, though it hasn't always been easy for her. At one meeting she befriended a Jewish lady. As they talked and shared together, they began to feel a sense of connection with each other. One evening as they were about to leave, the Jewish lady asked her to come outside to meet her husband waiting in the car.

Imm Basem took one look at the man and started to cry. She simply could not bring herself to shake hands with him—he was the captain who had come to her house years ago to arrest her son. The shock of seeing him again was overwhelming. Imm wept for hours.

Many Palestinians find it difficult to understand why the Jews, who probably know more about suffering than any other people in the world, impose such anger and hurt on them. "We love the Jews," some of them say, "but we hate the way they treat us!" As they have become acquainted with each other's heartache and gotten to know one another through such settings as *Musalaha*, hope for the future is dawning a little more brightly on the horizon.

Hours before we flew home to Holland, Johan and I spoke at the Baptist church in Jerusalem about persecuted believers worldwide. Afterwards, Alex Awad, who pastors there, asked the congregation to put into practice what they had heard. "Next week I want you to specifically pray for a country where people are suffering," he challenged us all. Some promised to pray for China, others chose Sudan, Algeria, North Korea, and Egypt.

I quietly resolved to pray for the suffering Palestinian Christians.

Palestinians are not usually persecuted for their faith *per se*, but they certainly are persecuted. They are made to feel like second-class citizens. They are continually humiliated simply because

---

[7]For more information on *Musalaha,* see Salim J. Munayer, ed., *Seeking and Pursuing Peace: the Process, the Pain, and the Product* (Jerusalem: Musalaha, 1998). Available from Musalaha, P.O. Box 52110, Jerusalem 91521, Israel.

of who they are. In many cases their houses and property have been taken from them without any form of compensation.

It has further hurt our Palestinian brothers and sisters to be neglected by the body of Christ worldwide. Because of our love for God's chosen people, the Jews, we have often forgotten that there are brothers and sisters in Christ among the Palestinians as well.

As I reflected upon all this, I began to pray that the Lord would help the Palestinian Christians overcome any anger and bitterness in their lives. "And Lord," I added, "please help Imm Basem and her family. Help them to know that in you they really do have a future and a hope."

# RACHEL

## "PAPA IS NOT HERE!"

Absently making small talk on their way to "church"—a house Christian fellowship they attended every Friday—Rachel and Wim were stopped at a traffic light in Riyadh, Saudi Arabia. Wim suddenly turned to his wife and said, "Rachel, when I get arrested, I want you to take the children home to Holland. Do it the way we planned."

CHAPTER 13

Wim's statement was made in such a matter-of-fact way that for an instant it sounded like a casual remark. But Rachel knew better. Wim hadn't said *if.* He'd said *when.*

"Oh no, Wim!" Rachel exclaimed. "Don't say that! God won't let that happen. And even if he did, I could never leave—I'd have to stay as close to you as possible."

Wim squeezed his wife's hand. "I know you'd want to stay. But I'd want you to go."

The two of them had always understood the potential consequences of working in Saudi Arabia. Wim was a businessman, but first and foremost he was a Christian. In Saudi that could mean trouble. As it turned out, for Wim it meant big trouble.

> "Because he loves me," says the Lord, "I will rescue him; I will protect him, for he acknowledges my name. He will call upon me, and I will answer him; I will be with him in trouble, I will deliver him and honor him. With long life will I satisfy him and show him my salvation"
>
> *Psalm 91:14-16*

## PRAYING FOR DELIVERANCE

A colleague and I were driving to a prayer meeting in Holland a few weeks later. "Oh, by the way," she told me. "Did you hear that Wim has been arrested in Saudi Arabia?"

My heart sank—we had heard the week before that two Filipino Christians had been put in jail for spreading literature. Was Wim's arrest related to that?

"Don't tell anybody yet!" my colleague cautioned. "It's too early to publicize his case. In fact, it may be that quiet diplomacy is a better option."

Within days nine more Filipinos were also arrested. Meanwhile, employees of the Dutch embassy in Riyadh had tried to visit Wim and had been denied entrance. The only good news was that Wim was being held by the Ministry of Internal Affairs and not the *Mutawa*, the brutal religious police. That was, for the moment, the only solid sign of hope.

During the weeks that followed, people across the globe took up the cause of Wim and the imprisoned Filipinos. Eventually the media got involved. Like many others, I prayed. I prayed during the day and during the night. I prayed in special prayer meetings and in private prayer times. I prayed while I was doing the dishes and bicycling to the market. Yes, I had even prayed during the World Cup Championship of Soccer.

The World Cup competition was taking place in France at the time. Everybody in Holland seemed to have caught the soccer bug, including me. But I could not help thinking of Wim. Like most Dutch people, he was a huge soccer fan.

Rachel and Wim are a Dutch couple, so Johan and I knew a bit about them and their background. Rachel had come to know the Lord as a young woman. Once she began her Christian life, she was eager to put her faith into action. A trained nurse for handicapped children, she jumped at the chance to work in a Christian orphanage on one of the Dutch islands in the Caribbean.

After a year Rachel returned to Holland, having learned more about humanitarian service than she'd bargained for. A few months later, she attended a missions banquet and found herself seated next to a young man who introduced himself as Wim. Even though they had both grown up in Holland's Noordoost polder, and their families did not live far apart geographically, they had never met before.

It was love at first sight. Both of them had been hoping, praying, and waiting for a mate who would also put Jesus first. The minute they laid eyes on one other, the search was over. With great joy and excitement, they both realized that they'd found the person of God's choosing. Two years later they were married in Emmeloord, the town where they first met.

Wim and Rachel studied Arabic in Jordan for a while. He had worked as an export manager in Saudi Arabia before meeting Rachel and had very much enjoyed his time there. Now, since he and Rachel were both able to speak Arabic, Wim was eager to return to Saudi. By then Wim and Rachel had two little boys, and the whole family applied for visas.

Wim's visa was granted immediately, but Rachel and the children's papers were not issued. Wim left alone, and Rachel and the kids stayed behind in Holland. Apart from taking care of her children, Rachel tried to make ends meet by working on Wim's parents' fruit farm.

Six months passed, and Wim began to suspect that he would never get permission to get his family to Jidda. Weary of the long separation, he changed jobs and moved to Riyadh. It was a good move because before long, the other visas were granted, and the family was reunited. Wim continued to work in the export business while Rachel took care of their children. Later on she was able to care for two Down's syndrome children, which allowed her to practice speaking Arabic and to use her special gift of caring for handicapped children.

## A Secret Plan

On a beautiful evening in 1995, Rachel and Wim were sitting in their car at the top of a hill overlooking the Riyadh city lights. As they prayed together, the Lord filled their hearts with a deep longing to reach the people of Riyadh with the gospel. They knew many Saudi people wanted to read the Bible, but it was absolutely forbidden and dangerous to give them a copy. Wim and Rachel had no idea how such a prayer could possibly be answered, but they prayed anyway.

They soon learned that a number of Filipino Christians also wanted to place the Word of God in the hands of the Saudi people. And these Filipinos had a very interesting idea—during the Gulf

War, thousands of Bibles had been stored in Saudi, and many copies were still there. Was there some way to secretly distribute them?

To help the Filipino Christians strategize a way to distribute the Bibles, some believers from abroad came for a visit. They knew the project could have deadly repercussions, so a long period of prayer was planned. It was essential that every person involved knew for sure that it was God's will for him or her to pass out copies of his Word in that very restricted country.

They decided to go ahead with the plan after about a year of intense prayer and planning. One early morning in June 1998, Filipino teams went out and hung parcels containing a Bible, a video of the life of Jesus, and information regarding Christian radio programs on five hundred doors in Riyadh. The packages could hardly be seen from the street because most of the houses had porches and gates.

Wim and Rachel were aware of what was happening. Rachel had had her doubts about the operation, but Wim felt that because the whole thing was so well thought out and covered in prayer, it might be God's way of reaching out to Saudis who otherwise would never hear the Good News. He knew the Filipinos involved were aware of the danger, but they were willing to pay the price for their actions.

It wasn't long before Wim heard about the first arrests.

"Some mistakes were made while the packages were distributed," he told Rachel. "The police were able to trace one of the cars to its Filipino owner."

Rachel shook her head sadly. "Even though I knew this could happen, I'm really upset at the thought of those people in jail. What do you think will happen to them? Will they be tortured?"

"I don't know, Rachel. If they are, some of them may be forced to pass on the names of other Christians in the city."

Wim and Rachel looked at each other. An unspoken question hung in the air. Would the imprisoned Filipinos mention Wim's name?

It was that same week that Wim reminded Rachel, "When they come and take me, I want you to go with the children to Holland for the summer, as planned." That Saturday, June 13, when Wim came home after picking up the kids from school, the police were waiting for him in front of his house.

They quickly surrounded the car. "We'd like to talk to you," one of them politely explained, "and we'd prefer to do it in the house."

Without further comment, they marched in and began looking through the house, room by room. Although the policemen were very friendly, and the atmosphere was relaxed, Rachel and the children kept themselves out of sight.

Wim took Rachel aside. "They're taking me somewhere," he calmly explained, "and they're promising that I'll be back in one hour. I think it will take longer. Here is a telephone number they gave me. Give it to our Saudi sponsor. Ask him to call."

Without another word, he hugged Rachel good-bye and disappeared with the police officers.

## WAITING FOR WORD

Rachel was stunned. Although she continually tried to reassure herself that everything would be all right, she felt lost in her own house, wandering from room to room, futilely awaiting Wim's return. After an hour he was not back. After twenty-four hours he still hadn't showed up. Their Saudi friend called the number Wim had been given, but they were not allowed to speak to Wim. "All I can tell you is that the Ministry of Interior Affairs made the arrest. I cannot disclose the prisoner's location to you at this time."

Rachel fared no better when she called. The first time, a man answered the phone and let her talk without saying a word. When she called again later, she was passed from one person to another, but still nobody was willing to tell her anything. Day after day she kept trying, repeating the same questions, "Can you please tell me where my husband is? I need some information about his case. What exactly is happening to him?"

None of Rachel's calls provided her with any information whatsoever.

Meanwhile, the house felt more empty and strange with every passing day. A sense of powerlessness crept into her consciousness.

Sometimes the phone rang at random times, and when she answered it, no one was there. Because this had also happened just before Wim's arrest, Rachel became increasingly concerned about the children's safety.

Fortunately, the children seemed to be fairly insulated during those days of uncertainty. They were still going to school when their father was taken, and their daily routine kept them busy. Once the summer holidays began and they had more time to miss Wim, Rachel took them to a water park, where they swam in the pool and played in the wave machine. They ended the day with french fries and ice cream. Although they were all acutely aware of Wim's absence, for a few hours, at least, life seemed almost normal.

Because of the phone calls and her own sense of foreboding, after twelve days Rachel decided to move in with friends. As Wim had instructed her to do, she began packing to go to Holland. But she was extremely reluctant to leave without him.

Rachel and her friends had a prayer meeting not long before she and the children were scheduled to fly to Amsterdam. "Lord," Rachel pleaded, tears flowing down her cheeks, "I cannot leave here without hearing from Wim. Please let me speak to him!" She was feeling more and more desperate to hear something—anything—about her husband. She couldn't bear the thought of being thousands of miles away from him without letting him know she was leaving, without knowing that he was all right.

On the morning of June 30, seventeen days after Wim had been arrested, Rachel was doing some last minute chores in her own house before leaving on some errands. Impulsively, she tried again to call. Like all the previous times, she was told that she could not speak to Wim. But this time the voice on the line said, "Maybe he will call you back."

Rachel gave the man her telephone number, seriously doubting that it would serve any purpose, and hung up. Five minutes later the phone rang. With her heart pounding, Rachel picked up the receiver. For the first time since their separation she heard the familiar voice of her husband.

"I can't talk to you very long, and we'll have to speak English. How are you? How are the children?"

They both knew others were listening to their conversation—probably recording it—so their conversation was rather stiff and awkward.

"We're all fine, Wim. The children are doing well. And I want you to know that we're packing," Rachel said, trying to choose her words as carefully as possible. "We're going on that trip you wanted us to make. But how are you? Are you okay?" Rachel's voice sounded high and strained.

"I'm being treated well. I'm having soup every day," he said with a slight chuckle.

Once she heard those words, Rachel knew Wim was doing all right. Wim loved soup, and they'd never had it for dinner quite as often as he would have liked. Telling Rachel he had soup every day was a subtle way of letting her know that he was being treated well.

The longer they talked, the more they struggled for words and fought off tears. After a few minutes, under the circumstances, there really wasn't much more to say.

"I guess I'd better hang up, Wim. Everyone is praying for you. The children send their love. I love you very much. . . ."

"I love you, too."

The conversation had been stilted and far too short, but after Rachel hung up the phone, she was overjoyed.

A huge burden had been lifted off her heart. She immediately called their families and friends. "I'm so thankful for a sign of life, for just hearing Wim's voice," she told a Dutch friend. "God *is* in control of our lives! He can be trusted. I've known and believed that all along. I'm just incredibly thankful that I was still in the house when the phone rang."

A couple of days later one of the Filipino prisoner's wives, due to have her first baby, was placed under house arrest. She delivered her baby while her husband was in detention. When Rachel heard about this situation, she was gripped with fear and panic. But the Spirit of God came to her rescue.

Out of the blue she began to hum an old Dutch hymn she hadn't thought of in years. Soon she was singing,

He is my rock and my Savior, He is my King and my Lord.
He is the one who can help me, that is what I experience all the
    time.

He gives me strength when I falter, sustains me when I succumb.
He is my light in the darkness, and that is why I feel rich.

As she sang, it wasn't long before the peace of the Lord came upon her, and her fear was gone. The Lord simply filled her heart with joy. She was so elated that she felt like dancing.

The children, sensing her joy, took each other's hands, and they all danced around the living room. Rachel lit candles, made pancakes, and prepared a special milk pudding from Holland for dessert. It was the happiest any of them had felt since Wim was taken away.

Rachel struggled in her decision of when to return home to Holland. She and the children had tickets for July 2, but both families in Holland were very worried about her and the children. They urged her to come home as soon as possible.

"They want me to change the tickets and leave earlier. But I have no peace," she told one of her friends. "What if Wim somehow comes home, and we aren't here to meet him? "

Their oldest son, Paul, felt the same way. When Rachel raised the possibility of leaving a week earlier, Paul burst into tears. "I don't want to leave yet!" he cried. "I want to be here when Papa comes!"

As July 2 approached, it became clear that Wim would not be coming home. Reluctantly Rachel decided to do what she had said she would do—leave for Holland. At least there the children would have family around.

Wim and Rachel owned a little holiday house in Holland. Whenever they came home for a vacation, it was there that they stayed. The place was familiar to the children, but when they walked through the door this time, Michael, the second son, exclaimed, "Papa is not here!"

*Strange*, Rachel told herself. *Somehow Wim's absence is more real to them in Holland than it was in Saudi.*

## CHRISTIANS IN ACTION

Sadness washed over her in waves during those first days in the Netherlands. Frightening questions interrupted her sleep with jarring urgency. Had she done the right thing in leaving Wim behind? Would she ever see her husband again?

As the news of the arrests became known, people in different parts of the world took action. Wim's family, their friends, and human rights organizations approached politicians in the United States, England, and Holland. Through quiet diplomacy, pressure was put on the Saudi government to release the prisoners. When Prince Abdul Aziz Bin Fahd was in Los Angeles for the opening of a large mosque (built at the expense of the Saudi Royal family), he was approached on behalf of the Christians in the Riyadh prison.

Despite all the efforts on the outside, no one knew what was going on inside the prison walls. What was really happening to Wim? Was he able to sense the prayers of Christians around the world?

Johan and I were able to visit Wim and Rachel in their home after Wim's release. In great excitement we drove through the scenic Dutch countryside to their house in the polder, anxious to give them a welcoming hug and learn the rest of the story.

With a smile on his face, Wim said, "If you want to know that God is real, have yourself locked up in a Saudi prison cell, and you'll soon find out! If ever I've felt God's presence, it was in that cell. As soon as I was locked up on that Saturday afternoon, I fell asleep. I slept soundly for several hours. When I awoke, I almost felt guilty. Everybody was bound to be worried about me, and here I was falling asleep!

"I was given sufficient food, and for the first seventeen days I was in a cell by myself. I was not allowed to have any contact with other prisoners, but the guards were friendly. The room was small, but air-conditioned."

One day a guard looked through the window in Wim's door, and Wim smiled at him. "How can you smile when you should be miserable, all by yourself in there?" the guard asked.

" I am not here alone—I have Jesus in my heart," Wim replied.

"It was the truth. I honestly didn't feel alone. In fact, I had a great time with the Lord in that cell with only a mattress, a pillow, and a camera in the corner. I had been very busy the weeks before I was arrested, and there hadn't been much time to spend alone with the Lord. Now I found myself in a situation where I had all the time in the world. I was totally dependent on God."

For hours Wim walked around his cell. He counted—seven steps from one wall to the other. He recited Scripture verses he had memorized—especially Psalm 68:19-20, the Scripture the pastor preached at Wim and Rachel's wedding. "Praise be to the Lord, to God our Savior, who daily bears our burdens. Our God is a God who saves; from the Sovereign Lord comes escape from death." God was indeed daily bearing Wim's burdens. And Wim firmly believed that God would deliver him from death.

Wim's main worry centered around Rachel and the children. He had no way of knowing how they were coping. He hoped and prayed that they would go to Holland, and when he was finally allowed to talk to Rachel and she told him she was packing, it put his mind at ease.

"The only time I was allowed out of my cell was for interrogation, and I was questioned for hours—one session lasted four hours. In the corner of the room in which I was interrogated, I saw instruments that could be used for torture. But they never used them on me. In fact, during those questioning times I really sensed the Lord's presence. He put the right answers in my mouth. My only fear was that I would cause harm to others.

A little strip of light coming into his room allowed Wim to keep track of night and day, and the calls to prayer from the local mosque helped him to know what time of day it was. On Fridays a whole sermon blasted through the loudspeakers of the mosque. When he heard that, he knew that it was the Muslims' day of rest.

## Answers to Prayer

"It was so obvious that people were praying for me. The Saudis are soccer freaks," Wim continued, "and the guards kept me informed about the results of the Dutch team. Once I was interrogated during a soccer match—South Korea vs. Holland. A guard promised to bring me a cup of tea every time the Dutch scored a goal. I had five cups of tea. Later, they let me watch Holland vs. Argentina, and I was told that it was one of the most interesting matches of the whole tournament."

"Thank you, Lord!" I could hardly contain my excitement.

"Wim, would you believe that during that same soccer match I specifically prayed for you? I was sad because I thought you were missing it, but you weren't, after all!" For me, that episode remains a great example of our Lord's interest in every detail of our lives, large or small.

"Did they ever try to convert you to Islam?" Johan asked.

Wim told us that he had been given Islamic literature to read. And when he was moved to another room, he found himself in the company of an Islamic professor, imprisoned because he was an "independent thinker," and an Egyptian Muslim. Both did their best to convert Wim to Islam.

"I was glad I had studied carefully the material they had given me. It came in handy when sharing my faith with them. They were willing to listen to me, but neither of them accepted Christ."

For Rachel, the last weekend before Wim's release proved to be the most difficult time of all. On July 5 she had been able to talk briefly to Wim—their second conversation by phone. Then, on Thursday, July 9, a friend called from the United States and told her that the prisoners would be released the very next day.

Rachel waited on pins and needles all day Friday. She waited on Saturday, too. No one called.

She flipped on the television and learned that a Dutch newspaper was reporting a dreadful story about an unidentified Dutch citizen who had been tortured in a Saudi jail. Fearing the worst, Rachel was seized by panic and struggled to maintain her faith and her composure.

"I kept thinking about 2 Corinthians 10:5," she told us. "'We demolish arguments and every pretension that sets itself up against the knowledge of God, and we take captive every thought to make it obedient to Christ.' For me, on that particular day, taking every thought captive was the hardest thing imaginable."

But the prayers, publicity, and diplomatic efforts on Wim's behalf finally bore fruit. At Open Doors we had a prayer meeting on Monday evening, July 13. It was Wim and Rachel's eighth wedding anniversary, and we prayed especially for them and their family, as well as for the Filipino Christians in prison.

Even as we prayed, Wim was on his way home.

Early the next morning Johan called me from his office. "Wim is free!" he told me. His words were music to my ears. I could hardly believe it. What a happy ending to this ordeal.

Or was it?

In one sense it was very good news indeed. Wim and Rachel were together, and the children had their father home. But there was also a sad consequence to all that happened. Wim was free, but he could never again work in Saudi Arabia. That door was closed. "Exit only" was stamped in his passport.

Wim's love for the Saudi Arabian people has not changed at all, in spite of his ordeal. "One month in prison cannot wipe out eight years of good experiences. We still love the Saudis," Wim told us. Rachel nodded in agreement.

"They are very friendly, hospitable people. Yet they seem to be prisoners of their own culture, and they need the freedom only Christ can give them. Many are hungry to hear about the gospel. Please pray that the Lord will continue to use the Bibles and videos that were distributed."

As we said good-bye, Wim put his arm around his petite wife. "One more thing has changed for the better," he said as he smiled and hugged her warmly. "Rachel is cooking a lot more soup these days."

# RUTH HUSSEIN

## CHRISTIANS IN A MUSLIM WORLD

At about eleven o'clock on a Monday morning, Ruth Hussein was bustling around the house, getting lunch ready for her husband, Mansour, who would be home momentarily. She absently glanced out the window at a bright spring day just in time to see a car pull up outside.

The doorbell rang, and when Ruth answered it, she saw three men standing outside—two police officers and her family's dear friend Harold, who was Mansour's coworker at the Christian bookstore.

Ruth's heart began to pound in her chest. It was beating so loudly that she could hear it in her ears. Her hands trembled with fear. Her thoughts fixed on Mansour and the death threats he had casually mentioned to her in recent weeks.

## CHAPTER 14

A father to the fatherless, a defender of widows, is God in his holy dwelling. God sets the lonely in families.

*Psalm 68:5-6*

"Come in," she said quietly, noticing Harold's pale and troubled face.

"We'd like to ask you a few questions," one officer began. "Does your husband owe anyone money? Does anyone owe him? Does he have any enemies that you know about?"

"As far as I know," Ruth said in a subdued voice, "he has no problems with anyone."

"Could it be that he's involved with another woman?"

Ruth was almost sickened by the question. "Why don't you ask him that yourself?" she answered curtly.

"We did ask him, but we just wanted to check with you."

Ruth's mind was racing. She couldn't seem to catch Harold's eye. Why wouldn't he look at her? "Why are you asking me all this?" she asked impatiently. "Is something wrong?"

"No, no, everything is fine."

Ruth knew very well that everything was not fine. Quaking with fear and enraged by the men's apparent indifference, she grabbed one of the police officers by the shirt with both hands and screamed at him. "You've got to tell me what happened!"

He backed up a step or two and said, "I'm sorry, madam. I'm sorry . . . but there's been a death."

Ruth turned to Harold, who looked at her helplessly. "Harold, is this true? Is Mansour dead?"

"Yes, Ruth." Harold's voice was barely a whisper. "What they've said is true."

Ruth quickly got their one-year-old son, Kevin, ready, rushed out of the house, frantically hailed a cab, and rode to her parents' home, where Mansour sometimes went to visit. Even though he was not there, Ruth still refused to believe what she had been told.

"The police say there's been a death," she told her sister, "But I don't believe them. I thought maybe he was here."

"No, he hasn't been here today. I think we should go to the hospital. If anything happened to him at all, he would probably be there," her sister said, picking up her handbag and heading for the door.

Several of Ruth's family members piled into the cab with her, all of them sick with worry. No one said a word as they drove through the busy streets.

The minute they parked, Ruth leaped out of the taxi and ran inside. "I'm looking for my husband," she explained to the attendant in the emergency room.

"His name, please?" the man asked, in an infuriatingly calm voice.

"Mansour Hussein."

He hesitated, looking at some papers. "Hussein. Oh yes . . . are you his next of kin?"

Ruth swallowed hard. "Yes. I'm his wife."

"Come with me then."

Ruth was led into the morgue, where she found herself staring at Mansour's corpse. There was no longer any doubt about what had happened. Ruth could see for herself the bullet holes in his body, and she was nearly immobilized with horror by what she saw. Only her mind was in motion, and it spun around frantically in search of answers: *Why would anyone want to kill Mansour? What terrible thing had he done to cause someone to want him dead? Who would do such a thing?*

Earlier that Monday morning, April 21, 1997, Mansour had eagerly headed out the door on his way to the Christian bookstore and library in Arbil, Kurdistan, where he worked. A man had phoned the night before, telling Mansour that he wanted to return a borrowed book early the next day. Always hoping for an opportunity to share the gospel, Mansour arrived long before the bookstore would normally open for business. He was quite willing to allow as much time as necessary for the unknown man to arrive.

Eventually, someone had showed up. But whoever went to the bookstore that morning did not go there to talk. Later that morning when Harold arrived at work, he found Mansour lying in a pool of blood, shot dead.

## SOUL MATES IN A SEARCH FOR TRUTH

From the earliest days of their friendship, Ruth had always been very impressed by Mansour, who was well known in their community as a gifted writer. Ruth Hussein was a teacher with a great love for history and literature, and she found great delight in reading Hussein's poetry. From the day they met, they spent many hours in animated conversation, searching together for the meaning of life.

As they got better acquainted, Ruth learned that Mansour had come from a tribe of Faily Kurds, who had originally lived along the Iran-Iraq border without any formal nationality. Born and raised in Baghdad, Mansour spoke only Arabic. He had graduated from a technical institute in the capital with a degree in survey engineering. For a time he'd worked in contract construction, partnering with his father and brothers. Then he left Baghdad in the early 1980s to work in Iran. While he was there, he took a good, close look at Islam, and he decided it wasn't for him. He had yet to find a faith of his own.

One day when Ruth went to the home of a colleague who taught in her school, Mansour was also visiting. He and Ruth had a short but interesting conversation about history, a subject in which they were both keenly interested. Ruth loaned Mansour a favorite book, and from that time on they were fast friends. As days turned into weeks, their friendship turned to love.

By that time everybody thought of Mansour as an atheist. In fact, his writings since his student days reflected Marxist ideals. But Communism did not answer his many questions; it did not satisfy the deep needs he felt inside. He was still looking for answers when he met a group of Christians in Arbil, and he bombarded them with questions.

"What makes Jesus so different from the other prophets? He was a good man—I know that. But what did he do that was so unique?"

"I guess being raised from the dead would be the primary thing," one of the men pointed out without a trace of irony. "But he also claimed to be God. He said he was one with the Father. The truth is, if Jesus wasn't God, he wasn't a good man, either. He was either insane, a liar, or who he said he was."

"Well, even if he was God, what's the difference between a good Muslim and a good Christian? They both fast. They both worship. They both pray. They both live morally. Why not just remain a Muslim?"

"There's one big difference," one of the women pointed out. "In Islam you are required to do certain things to reach paradise. The five pillars—well, you know all about that. But in Christianity, God does all the work for us. His death on the cross and his subsequent resurrection make it possible for us to be saved by grace, not by our own efforts. We have to believe in his work for us and then allow his Spirit to change our behavior from the inside out. Our works are *evidence* of our faith, but they aren't *a requirement* for salvation."

Mansour's curiosity was insatiable. He wanted to know about Jesus' identity, the Trinity, the Bible—so many things puzzled him. He spent hours talking with friends, and they patiently tried to help him understand. Finally, in January of 1996, Mansour's search ended, and he decided to surrender his life to Jesus Christ.

The change in him was immediate and dramatic. Joy and enthusiasm enlivened his quiet, reflective nature. He could hardly stop smiling. Ruth remembers those happy days so very well. It was not long before she, too, came to Christ, and from that time on they followed Jesus together. Their's was not an easy decision; they lived in a predominantly Muslim community. Mansour carried a pocket New Testament everywhere he went. Ruth vividly remembers how he would pull it out many times a day to study on his own or share its truth with others.

"Ruth, I'm convinced that we have found the Way, the Truth, and the Life," he told her one day.

"I am so sure, too," she said. "I've never experienced such peace and joy."

"It's not going to be easy," he warned her, "But as far as I'm concerned, there'll be no turning back."

"How could we turn back from Jesus, after all he's done for us?"

And so they committed themselves to seeing it through together—Christians in a Muslim world.

## THE WORST POSSIBLE NEWS

But now everything had changed. Mansour was gone. Their deep love for each other, their single-minded quest for spiritual growth and Christian understanding was forever lost. In its place were upheaval, confusion, and a heavy burden of sadness.

Ruth and Mansour had been married only a little more than two years, and Ruth's sense of loss was indescribable. She was without her husband, her closest friend. Kevin would now grow up without knowing his father. In the days that followed, Ruth was unable to eat or sleep or even to speak. Her desolation was acute. She felt completely alone with her thoughts, and those thoughts haunted her.

Sometimes she found a little comfort by holding Mansour's beloved New Testament in her hands—it had been found on the floor next to his body. The small, well-worn volume became one of Ruth's most cherished possessions. But her mind was not at rest. Grief overshadowed every aspect of her life.

In the traumatic days after the murder, friends supported Ruth and her little boy as best they could. They came to visit, to encourage, to console. As they all got together, it was no surprise that everyone seemed to have a special memory of her husband. One young man recalled Mansour's courage.

"Do you remember October 1996, when Saddam's troops invaded? Just about all of the other believers fled to Dohuk, but Mansour stubbornly refused to leave Arbil."

"Why should I be afraid?" he had asked his friends as they hurriedly waved good-bye to him. Privately, some of them thought he had lost his mind.

"Why wasn't he afraid?" Mansour's friend wondered aloud, shaking his head as he recounted the story. "He just wasn't. He was never afraid. Not at all."

"And he was always so kind to everybody," another friend commented. "He was forever telling somebody about Jesus Christ. But when they disagreed with him, mocked him, or even got angry at him, he never seemed to let it bother him. He was gentle and gracious, and he always treated people—no matter who they were—with the utmost courtesy."

"Do you remember the time," one woman recalled with a chuckle, "when he had the anesthetic?"

Everyone who had heard the story laughed.

During a medical treatment Mansour had been put under general anesthetic at a local hospital. "To the surprise of everyone who heard him," the woman concluded, "he started to sing and pray aloud in Jesus' name at the top of his lungs. You could hear him all over the hospital!"

As they all reminisced, Ruth and the others quietly acknowledged that Mansour had received death threats while working at the Christian bookstore. One man put into words what they all believed about Mansour's murder: "There is little doubt that Mansour died as a martyr. He gave his life testifying to the truth that is in Jesus. Clearly, that is why they killed him."

Not only was Ruth grieving the loss of her husband, she was also very worried about their friend Harold, who was the first person to enter the bookstore after the murder. Now he had been arrested. A Kurdish convert from Islam like Mansour, Harold had been accused of complicity in the crime and taken to prison.

Later on, Ruth was greatly relieved when she heard that Harold was released after nine days of interrogation. But Arbil was no longer a safe place for him to live. Fearing for his life, Harold began to move from place to place, rarely going anywhere alone. He had been a frequent guest in their home, and Ruth missed him. Although she knew he was grieving Mansour's death as she was, they could no longer communicate with each other. Harold was clearly in danger, and in that perilous region of the world, he had little choice but to run.

## KURDISTAN: A POLITICAL TIME BOMB

For decades the Kurds have been a forgotten, displaced people. When the western allies defeated Saddam Hussein's army and drove them out of Kuwait, the Iraqi Kurds profited from the chaos by proclaiming their independence. As yet, no state in the world has recognized Kurdistan, but it still exists because of the United Nations' obligation to protect the people living in the region.

Internal rivalry continues to jeopardize any safe haven for the Iraqi Kurds. The economic boycott against Iraq has taken its toll, and to make matters worse, Saddam Hussein has enforced an additional boycott against the Kurds in retaliation for their declaration of independence. This has devastated the economy in the region, and most people are unemployed.

Very few Kurds are Christians, and most of them remain unreached by the gospel. The majority of the Christians in the area belong to Armenian and Assyrian minority groups. Since there is a serious shortage of Bibles, Christian books, videos, and other Christian resources in the area, Open Doors teams have traveled the long road through Turkey to help the small Christian community in Kurdistan. That's how some of our colleagues came to know Mansour, and that's how we received word of how Ruth and her family were doing.

## A LETTER FROM RUTH

"It seems that the Lord has begun to lift from Ruth the burden of pain," one of her friends wrote to us about a month after Mansour's murder. "She has been playing with her son, Kevin, and was able to laugh with us when we visited her today. But we know how much pain still lies ahead.

"On May 7 Ruth discovered that she is expecting Mansour's second child. Pray that she and the baby will be kept healthy, and that the child will bring joy amidst all the sorrow."

In August 1997 one of our colleagues was granted a visa to enter Kurdistan again. Loaded with letters and cards from Christians all over the world, he visited Ruth and Kevin. With the help of different organizations, including Open Doors, she was able to move into her own house. Her mother began living with her, and through the church in Arbil, Ruth received additional assistance to help to take care of her family. Four months after the death of her husband, Ruth wrote to us:

> With my love and respect and on behalf of my son and my family, I thank you very much for your feelings which were shown in your letters and postcards sent to me after the accident of my husband, Mansour. I also thank you for your prayers and your help to us.
>
> I thank my Lord that he gave me brothers and sisters such as you in Holland and other countries. I hope you always remember us in your prayers to ask God to give Kevin (my son) and the coming baby health and power, and that he will help me to bring them up in a way that satisfies God, and to build a prospective future for them. I hope that one day I will be able to collect all their father's writings and know the result of the investigations of this case.
>
> I pray that this accident will not scare other believers and will not affect their faith. I pray that I meet my husband in the kingdom of God. Amen.

The bookstore in Arbil was closed for a while, but it opened again in December 1997. Ruth offered to help work there part-time, if necessary. But in her situation, her Christian friends strongly discouraged her from doing so.

Harold, Mansour's friend and coworker at the bookstore, left to study abroad. He had to flee his hometown because Mansour's killers probably considered him a witness to the crime, and he, too, might well have become an assassin's target.

# Bad Days for Kurdistan's Christians

The situation in northern Iraq has worsened since the death of Mansour. The border with Turkey is closed, and it is very difficult to enter the country from abroad. Only through Syria, with much difficulty, is it possible to reach Kurdistan. Courageous Christians continue to serve the Lord, but a lot of them, particularly the young, are fleeing. Muslim extremists are attacking Christian believers with increasing frequency.

Grace Community Church of Dohuk was attacked by a mob of hooligans. Its pastor, Yusuf Matti, was threatened with death unless he left the country. His children were traumatized, and the church was temporarily closed. Rival Kurdish factions increasingly terrorize evangelical Christians in an effort to cleanse the land of what they see as non-Kurdish elements.

Despite all this adversity, Christians continue to represent the cause of Christ with courage and tenacity, and their faithfulness makes it possible for the Kurdish people to hear the gospel. Recently, an Orthodox priest confided in one of our teams, "During the last three years, my people have been able to read more about God than during the past three centuries."

# "It Lightens My Burden"

About eight months after the death of Mansour Hussein, we received the good news that on the evening of December 26, 1997, Ruth, his wife, gave birth to a healthy baby boy. He weighed in at 7.7 pounds and she named him Danny. In Kurdish his name means "gift," as in 2 Corinthians 9:15 where it is written: "Thanks be to God for his indescribable gift!" The E-mail we received simply said, "Ruth is in good health and very thankful."

After Danny's birth one of our colleagues visited Ruth and her children again. As before, he was loaded with cards and presents from Christians everywhere. As she talked to our colleague, Ruth asked for specific prayer for her two little boys, and for herself, that she will be able to raise them in the best possible way. She requested prayer for her health, too—she has developed a kidney problem since Mansour's death.

Under Islamic law, Mansour's relatives have the right to take Ruth's sons from her and give them a Muslim upbringing. This is a very real threat, and it is our heartfelt prayer that it will not happen.

In a letter that our friend brought to us, Ruth thanked all the believers who remembered her in their prayers and showed their concern and affection through cards and letters. As before, she ended her letter by requesting prayer for others.

> I thank God for the local believers who help me a lot in caring for the children and raising them; they really encourage me spiritually and help me materially, so it lightens my burden. I would also like to ask prayer for the leading brothers here, who carry a lot of responsibility in spreading the Word.

Our prayers should certainly be with the people of Kurdistan. We should pray in particular for the courageous Christian leaders who work so faithfully there. We should remember Harold and his future.

But how can we pray for them without first praying for Ruth Hussein and her children?

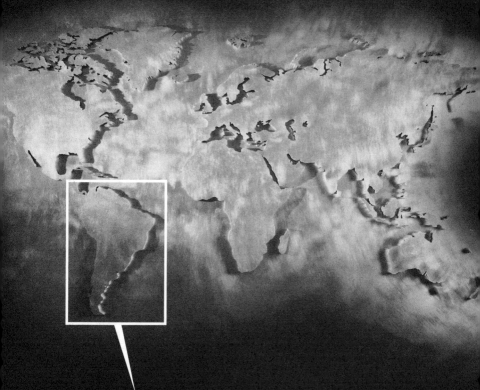

# SOUTH
# AMERICA

# MIRIAM AMADOR

## COURAGE FROM GOD ALONE

Along the northwest Colombian coast, the Atlantic seashore is lined with rustic cantinas and restaurants. Salsa and *vallenato* music blare out of aging speakers that hang suspended from palm-thatched roofs. The tropical air presses heavily against you with intense heat, and despite the upbeat music and free-flowing *cerveza*, the atmosphere is somber and menacing. The further inland you go into the Uraba region, the worse the mood gets. The jungle is dense, the terrain is rugged, and violence rules supreme. No one is exempt from its tyranny.

Colombia is a nation beset by anarchy. Warring factions confront each other in violent episodes that rarely make the North American news. The narcotics trade controls large sections of the country, while various guerrilla and paramilitary groups carry on an explosive power struggle. As a result, a violent death takes place every twenty minutes in Colombia, and 45 percent of the world's kidnappings occur there.

CHAPTER 15

Have I not commanded you? Be strong and courageous. Do not be terrified; do not be discouraged, for the Lord your God will be with you wherever you go.

*Joshua 1:9*

Against this backdrop, Christian believers are often caught in the crossfire between warring factions. They are targeted because of their courage in standing up for what is right. Their witness and evangelistic spirit are an obstacle to all those who want to live by their own rules: guerrillas, paramilitary forces, narco traffickers, common delinquents, and sometimes even the authorities.

## KILLED BY AN UNKNOWN ASSAILANT

Uraba is a place of horrendous suffering, particularly for evangelical Christians. In this one area alone, several pastors and church leaders as well as dozens of ordinary Christians have been murdered. Churches have been burned to the ground. Hundreds of believers have been dispossessed. Scores of women have been raped. Death threats have been regularly issued against pastors and missionaries who refuse to stop their evangelistic work.

In this remote area lives a pastor's widow named Miriam Amador. Her story is typical of countless others, and it underscores the need for prayer and practical help in Colombia. Miriam is a strong, sturdy woman with a wise face, who has seen more suffering in her life than she cares to remember. She and her children live under nearly intolerable conditions in a shed, a structure that bears more resemblance to a garage than a house.

Miriam didn't always live this way. After the death of her husband, she could no longer afford the family house, and she was forced to rent it out. Although she and her husband, Manuel, struggled for years to survive and to maintain a Christian presence in an unstable community, her worst troubles really began on July 12, 1995.

Manuel was late coming home that night, and Miriam glanced at the clock several times, fighting off uneasy feelings. As the minutes ticked by, her heart grew heavy with worry. She knew Manuel very well, and it wasn't like him to be late for dinner. Just as she glanced at the clock one last time, she heard gunshots. There were screams outside, and the sounds of people scurrying away in fear and confusion.

"Oh, God!" she cried. "I know it's him."

She rushed next door, pleading with the neighbors to tell her what had happened.

"I don't know what happened," said José, a good friend of the Amador family. "But you need to stay inside."

Miriam paused only briefly, unable to bear the uncertainty. In spite of José's objections, she went to see for herself what had happened.

The air was hot and sticky, and the village was gripped in an eerie silence. As she rounded a corner, praying every step of the way, all at once Miriam came upon her husband. He was lying on the ground, bleeding profusely from gunshot wounds.

"Manuel!" she cried, her heart breaking.

She took him in her arms, well aware that he was dying. "I love you, Manuel . . . ," she cried, holding him close, hoping he had some final words for her. But there were no words. In a heartbeat or two, he was gone.

Miriam's eyes searched the area. She scanned the darkness, hoping to catch sight of the gunman, but she saw no one. The street was empty. For the moment she knelt alone beside Manuel's body.

Grief and horror overpowered her. A cold chill spilled from her head down her body like an icy sheet. For a moment she thought she was going to faint. She vaguely wondered if perhaps she, too, were dying.

Miriam remained frozen in place. It seemed as if all existence had come to an end. Then gradually, slowly, she found the strength to make it home.

In the days that followed, Miriam was like a stranger to herself. She went through the motions of her life without feeling, without thinking. She felt as if she had lost all sense of being. She was unable even to handle the arrangements for Manuel's funeral; others had to do it for her.

## PASTOR MANUEL'S LAST WORDS

The night of the shooting, Ahimelic, Miriam's sixteen-year-old son, also found his way to the place where his father had been shot. As he gently examined the body, he found a letter in a blood-soaked pocket, which contained what turned out to be Manuel's final message. At a meeting scheduled to take place the following day, Manuel and other local church leaders had planned to send an SOS letter to the worldwide church regarding the senseless killings in Uraba. The letter was unfinished. Manuel was still developing one last point when he lost his life. The last paragraph read:

The day will come when you will see the difference between those that serve God and those that do not.

We have suffered the murder of men and women who were members of different churches in the Uraba region.

We are neither judges nor God to deplore and condemn the horrible death inflicted to our brethren, members of churches, missionaries, and pastors.

We only ask God that he, in his infinite love and mercy, grant forgiveness to those who raised their hands to kill our brothers, when they sincerely repent from their deeds and pray to God for forgiveness.

For Miriam, the days following the funeral were a blur. Visitors came and went, all of them reaffirming what Miriam already knew. Manuel was a beloved pastor and evangelist. He was known in the community as a Christian leader who loved everyone, believers in particular. Just about every person who came to see her asked Miriam the same question, "Why would they want to kill him?"

The answer was complex.

As bloodshed had increased in Manuel Amador's region, many professionals and businessmen began to flee. Manuel and most of the other pastors decided to stay, and this made them all the more vulnerable. In addition, Manuel had founded an evangelical Christian school in the area. This was much to the dismay of some traditional Roman Catholic authorities and the guerrilla fighters. They disapproved because a Christian education would teach children that violence was not God's way of solving problems. This, in turn, would lower the odds that the next generation would be easily recruited by terrorists.

## A STRUGGLE TO SURVIVE

After her husband's death, Miriam's life was thrown into upheaval. Not only did she lose her house, but a week after his father's death, her eldest son had to flee because of death threats against him. Ahimelec went to study for several months in Medellin, another of

Colombia's cities. Miriam grieved over his departure almost as if another death had occurred.

Although help from concerned believers is providing better housing for the family, Manuel's children are growing up without a father. And neighbors and other Christians are reluctant to help the Amadors because they fear retaliation from Manuel's killers. This only adds to Miriam's sorrow. It places her in a lonely, isolated position. And, grief or no grief, she now is the sole support for her family.

Miriam and some other widows started a small sewing shop. But in the face of continuing violence, the other women she worked with fled the area. When they moved out, they took the sewing machines with them. Fortunately, through some help she received from Christians, Miriam was able to buy a new sewing machine. She can now at least continue to provide for her family.

Miriam's struggle to survive as a widow continues. And, tragically, she is far from being the only one. Other Colombian pastors' widows have described to us the despair of their children—who have seen their fathers killed before their eyes. One especially painful example was the story of a woman named Dora Vallejo. Not only was her husband killed, but her sixteen-year old daughter was raped, a crime that resulted in a pregnancy. Apart from coping with her own deep sorrow, Dora had to deal with her daughter's unspeakable trauma.

An Open Doors team recently went to visit Miriam. "I wish you could have been there, Anneke," one colleague told me. "Miriam Amador needs so much prayer. I told her about you and about the book you're writing. I assured her that you would ask others as well to pray for her."

Visiting Miriam was virtually impossible for me. Even for the men who went, men who are accustomed to such things, getting to her was a dangerous enterprise. A local pastor, Brother Gustavo, agreed to accompany them on their visit.

"It won't be easy," he explained to them. "If we hire a taxi in town, we could be traced, and I would be punished by guerrillas or paramilitary thugs for taking foreigners around."

Gustavo thought long and hard before deciding what to do. Finally, he suggested that they take a bus to a town about twelve miles away, where Gustavo was not known. There they would hire a taxi to take them to Chigorodo, the town where Manuel Amador had pastored the Foursquare Church.

The trip proved to be both risky and frightening. On the way the taxi driver suddenly made a screeching U-turn and sped away in the opposite direction.

"Why did you do that?" one of the men asked.

"Señor, there has been no traffic coming from the opposite direction for more than ten minutes. That probably means there's a guerrilla roadblock ahead. That is very dangerous for you. I turned around in order to take a different road."

Traveling in that area was a high-risk enterprise—guerrillas were all around. After that particular incident, the team was even more thankful that Pastor Gustavo had been willing to come along. He knew his way around.

Despite the hair-raising cab drive, the foursome eventually arrived safely at their destination. They located Miriam and her family and were able to sit and talk with them. Despite her grief, they could quickly see that she continued to trust in the Lord. Life was not easy for her, and the future was fraught with danger.

"Out here," she told them, "it seems like the enemy continually wants to destroy God's plans and destroy each of us. He uses the violence around us and the grief we have to cope with constantly. But I try to keep my eyes fixed on Jesus, the author and finisher of our faith. That is carrying me through—focusing on Jesus, and not on the circumstances."

Because of her experience in operating a small clothing shop, Miriam had been asked to go and train some women in another town. But the road to that town was very dangerous; two buses had been burned and five people killed on that route.

"What am I to do?" Miriam asked our coworkers. "I have to give the businessmen an answer soon, but I don't know what to say because I am so terrified to travel on that road. If I go, I may never come back, and my children will be all alone. If I don't go, I could miss a very important opportunity. That's how we live, in that kind of tension."

# STRONGER THAN GUNS

The shining stars in Miriam's world are her children. Her son Ahimelec is a particular source of pride and joy, having returned home from Medallin. Before the death of his father Ahimelec dreamed of having a career and making money. Now, at eighteen years of age and still a student, he has a different purpose in life.

"If the death of leaders helps the church to grow, it is worth the cost," Ahimelec told the team. "That kind of courage can only come from God. I believe God is giving me the courage to help many young people to follow Christ. I want to tell them that it is not weapons that give them a way out. There is someone stronger than guns."

When Miriam was asked how Christians around the world can best help her and the other believers in Uraba, she didn't have to think long for an answer.

"Ask them to support us with their prayers. The enemy continually wants to destroy God's plans, and he wants to destroy each of us. In this country, when a person comes to Christ, Satan tries to stir up persecution and violent incidents to keep him from going forward and growing in grace.

"Pray for us, that we may continue to be strong, always keeping in mind God's promise to us in Joshua 1:9: 'Have I not commanded you? Be strong and courageous. Do not be terrified; do not be discouraged, for the Lord your God will be with you wherever you go.'

"That is my hope and confidence, and that is why I have remained here in Uraba, despite the violence," Miriam explained to her visitors. "We have been pressured to investigate various people in regard to the death of my husband. My response has been that we trust in a loving God, who is just and faithful. We do not live for vengeance. We live only to serve the Lord."

# PELAGIA SALCEDO

## NO TURNING BACK

"So how was your trip?" I asked my husband once we had stuffed his luggage into the trunk and headed home from the airport. Tired as he was, I could see that Johan wanted to talk.

He gave me a coy look and smiled. "I hope you don't mind, but while I was gone, I hugged another woman. . . ."

CHAPTER

"Come, follow me," Jesus said, "and I will make you fishers of men."

*Mark 1:17*

Johan had just returned from a trip to Peru, and once I heard the details of his meeting with the female prisoners in Lima's Santa Monica women's prison, I didn't mind in the least that he'd given that other woman a hug. In fact, I was more than happy he'd been able to let Pelagia Salcedo know that Western Christians care about her ordeal and are praying for her.

Like Colombia, Peru has faced its share of turmoil and violence in the past few decades. It's a place where trouble can erupt unexpectedly and without warning. In 1994 Pelagia Salcedo's life was shattered when she and her husband were suddenly arrested, sentenced, and imprisoned on trumped-up charges of terrorism.

Early one December morning, hours before daybreak, Pelagia was awakened by an unfamiliar sound. At first she'd thought it was another bad dream—it wasn't unusual for her to have nightmares about the police raids that threaten nearly everyone in Peru—but this was no dream. The sound she heard was all too real. All at once several heavily armed police officers were shoving their way into the Salcedos' bedroom.

Pelagia watched in silent horror as the heavy-handed officers pulled her husband out of bed, threw him on the floor, kicked him repeatedly, and pulled a hood over his head. One of them then grabbed her by the arm and dragged her outside, too. Without explanation, the Salcedos were shoved into a waiting police car and driven to the *Dincote*, Peru's National Anti-Terrorism Headquarters.

For hours Pelagio and Juan Carlos were interrogated, sometimes alone and sometimes together. Now and then, while she was being questioned in a separate area, Pelagio could hear the sound of her husband's tortured voice, screaming in pain.

"Oh, God, help him. Help us both! Jesus, have mercy on us!" She murmured the prayer continually, tears pouring down her face.

The Salcedos were held for about a week before they were brought before one of Peru's infamous "faceless judges." Under this cruel system, men with their faces covered to avoid identification have the power to legally bypass the normal judicial process. This is purportedly done to stamp out terrorism. In reality, it is a form of terrorism itself.

As Juan Carlos and Pelagia stood bound before him, the judge coldly sentenced Juan Carlos to be locked up at a men's prison in the Andes. Pelagia would be sent to Lima, to the Santa Monica prison.

Both Pelagia and Juan Carlos were given thirty-year sentences.

When Pelagia heard "thirty years" she began to scream. Until then, she had managed to restrain herself, praying and hoping for the best. But in the terrible moment, she was overwhelmed with desperation and hysteria. The police had dragged her away from her two children, who were at home alone without anyone to care for them. Now, as she realized that her husband was about to be led away from her for good and that they might never see each other again, Pelagia lost all control of her emotions. She collapsed, choking on her tears.

Juan Carlos was able to get to her side for one last moment, and he did what he could to comfort her. "Don't worry, my love," he said, his voice breaking, "These people are not Christians. They know nothing about the justice of God. *Our God is just.*"

Pelagia could find little comfort in her husband's words. All she could think about were their children. And as if that weren't enough, she watched helplessly as her beloved Juan Carlos was led away, perhaps forever, to his prison in the Andes.

She, in turn, was driven to her own final destination at Santa Monica. "You'll never come out of here alive!" the guards shouted. As Pelagia heard the echo of the prison door clanking shut behind her, she cried out to God: "Blessed Father, you know I am innocent. Please don't allow those words to be fulfilled."

## NO WAY OUT

How can innocent people like Pelagia and Juan Carlos be arrested and sentenced to thirty years in prison without a proper trial? What lies behind the ongoing political tragedy in Peru? The answers are both complicated and confusing.

In 1970 Abimael Guzman, a former philosophy professor, founded a terrorist organization called the Shining Path (*Sendero Luminoso*). The idea of violent class struggle working toward a peasant-based agrarian society won many converts among poor peasants long neglected by the Peruvian government. Since 1970 tens of thousands of innocent people have been killed in that "violent class struggle." Guzman was finally arrested in 1992, but in several regions of Peru, his violent guerrilla factions continue to cause misery and suffering.

Unexplainably the Christian community often has become a particular target. Caught between terrorists and the government troops, many believers have been falsely accused of terrorist activities. Pelagia and her husband are just two of the more than two hundred evangelical Christians arrested on false charges. The simple act of handing a glass of water to a guerrilla fighter—while having a gun pointed at them—was the only crime some of the imprisoned Christians ever committed.

Not only are the laws unjust, but the prisons of Peru are incredibly inhumane. There is absolutely no way out of them—they are virtually inescapable, and the sanitary conditions are appalling. Most cells are only six by ten feet square. A small, uncovered hole is dug out into the corner of each cell to serve as a toilet. The food is nearly inedible—it often contains cockroaches or pieces of broken glass. Two or three inmates share a cell. If all goes well, they are taken outside for half an hour of daylight. Perhaps worst of all, they have no idea what the future will bring.

Pelagia and the other women tried to make the best of their terrible circumstances. In spite of everything, somehow Pelagia still continued to follow the Lord. She was eventually selected by her fellow prisoners to serve as their Christian service coordinator.

It was when an Open Doors team visited Pelagia in prison that Johan had the opportunity to meet her. The women were so grateful for the visit. The team was taken to the prison courtyard, and one by one the Christian inmates were brought out. They were just as glad to see each other as they were to meet their visitors. Everyone stood in a circle and talked for a while. Pelagia spoke of how broken she had been after receiving her sentence, how she'd felt God had abandoned her.

"Finally I prayed, *Lord, please, speak to me! Please say something to make me feel better!* When I opened my Bible, I found myself reading Isaiah 41:10: "Do not fear, for I am with you; do not be dismayed, for I am your God." In that moment I knew that God would never leave me. He was in here with me."

Thus encouraged, Pelagia started sharing the gospel with the other prisoners. Some listened to her. Others laughed at her. A few accepted Christ.

The Open Doors team and the women all prayed together. Then Pelagia proposed that they sing a song. Despite their severe surroundings and their uncertain future, the little gathering of Christians began to sing an old familiar chorus: "I have decided to follow Jesus, no turning back, no turning back." By the time the song was over, everyone was weeping.

Johan put his arm around Pelagia's shoulder and quietly prayed for her. How she must have been longing for her husband's embrace. As that brief prayer ended, the guards indicated that it was time for the visitors to be on their way.

## FREE BUT FRUSTRATED

In August 1996 the Peruvian Congress passed a "Pardon Law." This resulted in the release of many evangelical prisoners and others who were imprisoned under false charges of guerrilla activity. Even though the Peruvian government did not admit to having made mistakes (the Christians were only "pardoned"), the law was a clear answer to prayer for thousands of people around the world who had long prayed for Peru's imprisoned believers. Since 1996, although some Christians still remain in prison, more and more have gradually been released.

On Friday, October 4, 1996, after almost two years, Pelagia regained her freedom. "I will never forget that day," she said later. "As I walked through the gates of the Santa Monica prison, I saw my precious daughter, Marlene, waiting for me in the bright sunshine. We cried as we hugged each other. And this time, at last, we were crying tears of joy and not of despair."

Pelagia was driven to the house of a sister-in-law, where her son, Abilio, was waiting for her. Pelagia had not seen him for two years. Despite the happiness Pelagia felt in her newfound freedom, it was a difficult reunion.

Abilio had given up visiting his mother in prison. He had been deeply affected by his parents' imprisonments, primarily because he had been told that they were guilty and that he would probably never see them alive again. The boy had resigned himself to living as an orphan. He had hardened his heart to keep it from breaking.

The news of Pelagia and Juan Carlos's impending release caught Abilio unprepared. He simply couldn't cope with meeting his mother at the prison gates. Now, when she actually walked into the room, he threw his arms around her and wept.

The following Sunday, Juan Carlos returned home, too. Pelagia had not seen him for two years. She watched from a distance as he walked down the gangway from his plane, and at first she didn't recognize him. But Juan Carlos certainly recognized Pelagia. He managed to hold back his tears until they were able to hold each other. Then, weeping openly, they embraced one another as if they would never let go.

Marlene, too, clung to her parents and cried. She and her brother had been separated during their parents' imprisonments, each living with one of their aunts. They had been able to see each other fairly often, but they had led very different lives.

Although the family was finally reunited, it was not the end of

Pelagia's heartache. She and Juan Carlos struggled to rebuild their relationship with their children. Both Marlene and Abilio had been told lies about their parents, and those oft-repeated stories had turned the children against them. No matter how hard Pelagia and Juan Carlos worked or what they said to renew the affection, love, and respect that had been lost, their efforts seemed to fall on deaf ears.

Quite simply, the children had planned their lives in ways that left no room for their parents. And sometimes, to Pelagia, her son and daughter seemed like strangers. She had longed for them for two years, and now they didn't seem to want her around. The ache in her heart was piercing. How could her own flesh and blood reject her? She had longed for them so much. Their estrangement was more punishing than her years in prison.

Pelagia isn't the only one who has experienced this problem. Often the greatest test for the wives of persecuted Christian men involves their children. The enemy seems to target the young for his most aggressive assaults. The process of rebuilding parent-child relationships sometimes seems to extend far beyond the years of imprisonment or mourning. As we pray for the wives of persecuted men and for the struggles of persecuted women, we should never fail or forget to pray for their children.

## "My Beloved Wife . . ."

Thankfully for Pelagia, the love of her husband, Juan Carlos, is a great and lasting comfort. One day, while in isolation in his prison cell, he wrote a poem to his wife:

> I'm grateful my love
> For the silver moon of your years
> For the love you express in silence
> For tenderness without deceit
> For patience, my beloved wife
> Thank you my love
> For being the fertile ground to my children
> My guitar in moons of autumn
> My great companion in loneliness

And the source of my happiness
Thank you my love
For providing the fragrance of your love
The purity of your heart
Your tender understanding
And a reason to exist
Thank you my love
Thank you my wife
Thank you my Pelagia

Deep in their hearts, the Salcedos knew that their love would carry them through. Together they vowed to fight for their son and daughter. They resolved to do whatever they must to regain their children's love and respect, and they knew that prayer was one of their most important weapons. So even after they left prison, they continued to ask for prayer for their family. They longed to be the happy, affectionate family they had once been.

God sometimes responds to prayer in the most unexpected ways. Pelagia and Juan Carlos's answer began to unfold when a Scottish film crew arrived in Peru to interview the Salcedos about their prison experiences. The children saw the love and respect their parents were shown by the Christian filmmakers and the accompanying team. These people were treating their parents with respect. Maybe it would be a good idea to take a second look at things from a different perspective.

Gradually the children were able to understand that their parents were not bad people after all. They finally came to believe that Pelagia and Juan Carlos had been innocent from the start. Today Abilio has left school to help Juan Carlos rebuild the family business. Marlene is working hard to finish high school so she can study journalism. The Salcedos are well on their way to renewing the godly, laughter-filled home they once shared.

Pelagia and Juan Carlos reassure everyone who visits them that they have only one desire—to continue to serve the Lord. As far as they are concerned, their work in Peru has only just begun. They seek our prayers and they long for our friendship. But in prison or out, come what may, they will continue singing—and living—the song that best describes their Christian journey:

## PELAGIA SALCEDO

We have decided to follow Jesus,
We have decided to follow Jesus,
We have decided to follow Jesus,
No turning back, no turning back!

# ROSA OCALDO

"If my parents hadn't given Satan the battle they did—if they hadn't stood in the gap for me—I am sure of this one thing: Today I would be dead."

CHAPTER

He will be a spirit of justice to him who sits in judgment, a source of strength to those who turn back the battle at the gate.

*Isaiah 28:6*

Adriana's face was solemn as she spoke, and there was no question about the sincerity of her words. She and her parents had traveled many miles to speak at a church in Virginia, and even though she was only sixteen years old, the poised young woman did not seem shy or intimidated. The church building was certainly a lot bigger and nicer than anything she'd seen in Colombia, and the people were dressed more expensively, but Adriana had a message to share, and that's where she kept her focus.

From the time of her arrival in North America, it hadn't taken Adriana long to learn that young people in the United States are tempted, too, by music, friends, alcohol, and drugs. Satan has many ways of influencing Christians of all ages. Because of his relentless attacks, Adriana had known a time when her own life was a living hell. Now she refused to miss an opportunity to talk about Jesus—the one who had delivered her.

As she listened to her oldest daughter's testimony, "Rosa Ocaldo's" eyes filled with tears of gratitude. It was still hard to believe that this was her Adriana speaking. So short a time before, her daughter had been a very different girl. Under the influence of Satan worshipers, her little girl had turned into a wild and belligerent teenager.

As she leaned back in her chair, Rosa quietly took her husband José's hand. At that moment words were not necessary between them. She knew he felt exactly the same way as they watched parents and children all around them being touched by Adriana's story. It was wonderful to see how beautifully the Lord was using their daughter's testimony, especially after all they'd been through together.

## TIMES OF TROUBLE

José and Rosa Ocaldo and their daughters, Adriana and Patricia, are missionaries, but they did not travel to a foreign land to share the gospel. Instead, they stayed in the country where they were born and raised. They chose to serve the Lord in Colombia.

Besides having planted and pastored several churches, they also established a growing mission to unreached indigenous groups in their country. Over the course of many years, they made countless missionary journeys during which, for periods ranging from one week to seven months, they lived among various tribes. As a result, the Ocaldos established a cross-cultural training school, where they train future missionaries to work with Colombia's ethnic minority groups.

Their ministry has flourished despite the dangerous conditions in their land—Colombia is certainly dangerous. Because of the political situation and the presence of many different warring factions, violence abounds. Travel is hazardous. Rebels and paramilitary groups infest the countryside, putting up roadblocks at random. The Ocaldos have faced nerve-shattering ordeals throughout their years of ministry.

Some years ago, for example, they were stopped by a group of heavily armed guerrillas. "You come with me!" a soldier commanded as he firmly gripped Rosa's arm.

"Please, let me stay with my husband!" she screamed as she saw another soldier leading José away.

For about three hours the two of them were interrogated at different locations.

*Please, Lord, help me!* Rosa prayed in desperation, while she tried to give truthful answers to the questions asked. The rough-looking rebels standing in front of her were very intimidating, but still she persisted in her prayers. Eventually the ordeal stopped, and she was reunited with her husband.

"You're just lucky!" the rebel commander said to Rosa with a smirk. "Both of you answered the questions in the same way. If you had answered three incorrectly, we would have killed you, because lying means you are an enemy agent. If you had answered two incorrectly, we would have kidnapped you. Get out of here now before I change my mind!"

He didn't have to say it twice. José and Rosa raced to their car, trembling with relief and praising the Lord together as they continued their journey. Characteristically, their close call didn't hinder José and his coworkers from continuing to distribute Christian literature in areas rife with kidnapping and murder.

From the start Rosa was very much involved in the work. On many occasions she traveled with José and other team members to visit the indigenous people and provide medical help and pastoral care for them. She went along when the team held literacy training and vocation Bible schools in different areas of the country. She supported José when he spoke at conferences in different cities.

Over many years Rosa watched as the political situation in their country deteriorated. So many different violent groups were fighting each other to gain control, it was nearly impossible to know one faction from another. Christians who refused to take sides in the conflict or to use weapons and violence were squeezed from all sides because of their neutrality. At times they paid dearly for it.

## DEATH THREATS

More than once the Ocaldo family crossed guerrilla territory in a canoe with an outboard motor. One false move would have made them prey to either the piranhas in the water or the violent authorities on either side of the shore. José and Rosa sometimes hiked through the jungle for hours, passing man-eating anacondas and lakes of quicksand that could have swallowed them alive.

During one particular ministry expedition, native guides

brought José and Rosa to a tribal land next to a waterfall. The Indians told them they could no longer accompany José and Rosa beyond that point because the shamans had placed a curse of death upon anyone who went farther. With firm conviction, Rosa led a time of prayer in which she asked that God's power be manifest over the curse. The group continued its mission trip, made contact with a tribe, and for the first time the natives of this area were able to say, "There is a greater God than ours!"

For a while José was warned repeatedly that if he did not stop his evangelistic activities, he and his family would pay with their lives. The threats were delivered by letter and by anonymous voices on the phone. At one point José was so alarmed that he decided to take his family and flee to the jungle.

"Mommy, where are we going?" Patricia asked again and again as the miles sped by. "I want to go home!" Afraid to worry them, Rosa had not forewarned the two little girls. Instead, she and José had picked them up after school. When the girls got into the car, their packed suitcases were awaiting them.

"We can't go home tonight, darling," Rosa said, smiling to calm her youngest daughter.

"We're going on a camping trip!" José interrupted, trying to sound as excited as possible.

But the "camping trip" was too hard and too long to be fun. José was afraid to stay long in any one place, so for weeks the family slept out in the open and wandered. They fed themselves with berries and roots, occasionally daring to buy food in outlying villages.

All of José's careful maneuvers proved unsuccessful. Several weeks after the family returned home, they received a letter. It described in detail their daily activities during the days they had been "in hiding." Someone had followed them, watching their every move. The letter ended with yet another threat. "We will kill you if you don't stop your travels. This country does not need the message you preach."

As it turned out, however, the battle that raged within the Ocaldos' own household was fiercer than anything they ever encountered outside.

## THE BATTLE WITHIN THE GATE

No matter how difficult life became outside their home, Adriana and Patricia were the apples of their parents' eyes. "Our daughters caused us nothing but joy for many years," Rosa remembered. "We never received any complaints from the school they attended. On the contrary, we were praised for their behavior. We thought that, as parents, we were doing quite a good job raising them."

But all of that changed when Adriana became a teenager. From a sweet little girl, she turned into an angry and disobedient rebel. She spent much of her time in her bedroom with the door closed. She spent hours on the phone talking to people her parents did not know.

All of this changed behavior drove her parents to their knees. Even though Rosa realized that some of Adriana's conduct was typical of girls Adriana's age, she sensed that deeper, more sinister things were happening to her little girl. A war seemed to be raging, and it did not appear to be a matter of "flesh and blood."

All Rosa and José knew to do was pray, and pray they did. "Please, Lord, show us what to do! Give us wisdom. Guide us. And Lord, please, please touch her!" Sometimes they could no longer find words for their prayers. When that happened, they simply wept for their troubled child.

As time went by, Rosa became aware that there were active Satanists in their neighborhood. Newspaper articles and television programs confirmed her suspicions. There were innumerable news items regarding these groups' dark influences in Colombia's society. Reportedly, little children had been kidnapped never to return.

One afternoon Rosa and José returned home after taking a visitor to the airport. Contrary to their house rules, Adriana had invited a young man into their house while they were away. Sensing that this person had a negative influence on Adriana, José asked the unwelcome friend to leave the house. "You can throw me out of your house," he protested, "but I assure you that your daughter belongs to us. She already belongs to Satan, and we will prove it to you." Slamming the door behind him, he left.

Previously Adriana had refused to talk to her parents about her new friends, but now she was willing to open up. Shocked and trembling, she started to talk. "For a long time now Alex has wanted to invite me to the Satanist church, but he has always encountered an obstacle. He said that you are the ones who stand in their way." Rosa remembered the many hours she and José had been awake at night, praying for their daughter. Adriana's words made sense.

One night during a sleepover with a relative, Adriana disappeared. José's concerned brother called and said that he had given Adriana and her cousin permission to go out for a few hours that evening, but that Adriana had refused to return. "She wants to stay at the party," he said. He passed on the address where their daughter was located. Rosa was startled; it was the house belonging to the Satanists, just a few houses down the road from them.

Adriana had behaved so well that day. She was unusually pleasant to her parents and little sister. Looking forward to a quiet evening, Rosa had given her permission to sleep over with her cousin. "I'll never forgive myself for this," Rosa muttered, as she and José quickly dressed and went outside to find their daughter.

A man of about fifty-five stood at the entrance of the house. "We have come to get our daughter," José informed him. The man said that Adriana had left, and he refused them entrance. A young man then came out of the house, and Rosa and José asked him if he had seen Adriana. "She's gone," he confirmed. "She left with some friends, and she was drunk."

Not knowing quite what to do, Rosa and José returned home to ask the Lord for further guidance. After some time, they both felt that their daughter was still in the house. They went and tried again, but the guard would not let them in. Desperate, José convinced a police patrol car to stop. When the police asked for permission to enter the house, the guard gave in, but only Rosa could accompany him. José had to stay outside.

As she went from room to room searching for her daughter, Rosa's worst fears came true. She could only see the silhouettes of young people dancing, some slamming themselves against the walls and into each other. There was a lot of liquor and the smell of hallucinogenic substances. She figured that at least eighty people were there. But she did not find Adriana. Everybody she asked told her that Adriana had left.

Outside the house, José's brothers had joined him. Rosa told them what she had seen. Just when they were about to go home, a bunch of people left the house, shouting and screaming, "You ruined our party!" To Rosa and José's astonishment, they noticed Adriana in the middle of the group. She seemed angrier than most of them, shouting degrading words at her father. José, indignant and angry, grabbed his daughter by the arm and tried to put her in the police car. Adriana kicked and screamed, putting up a fight and trying to break loose. Rosa grabbed her feet. "In the name of Jesus, obey!" she shouted. Adriana seemed to lose her strength, and they got her into the car.

Angry because they had lost their prey, the crowd raised their fists to hit José and Rosa. "You don't have the right to take your daughter," they threatened. "We will get back at you!" But the Ocaldos knew a major battle had been won. During the previous months, they had learned a lot about spiritual warfare. And they realized their God was stronger than the forces of the enemy.

The battle that followed was intense, but Rosa wasn't about to give Adriana up. The girl belonged to Jesus, and her mother knew that his power was stronger than any demonic force. Many sleepless nights followed— nights spent in prayer and spiritual warfare.

Sometimes Rosa grew so weary that she felt she could not go on, and at times she and José wondered if they shouldn't simply give up their ministry and leave the country. They realized that the work they were involved in was robbing Satan of his ancestral altars among the indigenous peoples. Guerrilla fighters were being changed by the power of Christ. Others were being prepared and trained for effective evangelism. Satan was angry, trying to divert their attention and wear them out so they would be useless for the ministry to which God had called them. What better way to distract them than to attack their beloved daughter?

In desperation one afternoon, Rosa prayed, "Lord, please give me a sign that you are with us and that our daughters belong to you." She opened her Bible randomly, and some words seemed to leap off the page and into her heart.

> Can plunder be taken from warriors, or captives rescued from the fierce? But this is what the Lord says: "Yes, captives will be taken from warriors, and plunder retrieved from the fierce; I will contend

with those who contend with you, and your children I will save. I will make your oppressors eat their own flesh; they will be drunk with their own blood, as with wine. Then all mankind will know that I, the Lord, am your Savior, your Redeemer, the Mighty One of Jacob" (Isaiah 49:24-26).

Hope surged through Rosa, and encouragement warmed her soul. She gained new strength in but a moment's time. Why? Because she understood that the "plunder" spoken about was her daughter. And she knew right then and there that God would not let the enemy take Adriana away.

Gradually, Rosa and José began to see a change in their daughter. She became more docile and friendly. The most critical time was always on Fridays and Saturdays, when Adriana wanted to do things and go to places that her parents would not allow. Then new attacks of rebellion and hysteria would occur. By the time Adriana was fifteen, however, the worst seemed to be over, although it took a long time before the restoration process was complete. But just then, yet another crisis came into their lives.

## An Unwelcome Gift

"Look, Mom! Somebody brought us a present!"

Excitedly, Patricia handed the gift-wrapped box to Rosa. The family had just finished their daily devotional, but instead of feeling the usual peace God's Word provided, Rosa felt anxious. *Strange,* she thought as she turned the package around in her hands, *it's no one's birthday, and there's no indication as to who sent it.*

"Did you recognize the man who gave you the present, Patricia?" she asked her daughter.

"No, I've never seen him before. But c'mon, Mom, open it! I want to know what's inside!" Impatiently, Patricia bounced up and down around her mother. Like all young girls, she loved presents.

Rosa shook her head. "Let's ask Daddy first," she insisted.

As always, José was on his guard. So much had happened to his family in recent months that he found it hard to trust anyone. "Let's have an authority look at it," he decided despite his daughter's complaints. It proved to be a wise move. Upon examination, the box was found to contain a hand grenade set to explode the instant the package was opened.

Rosa didn't sleep at all that night. As she relived the family's close call, she became more and more worried.

"Lord, I knew serving you would not be a picnic, but this is not what I expected when I married José," she cried quietly, afraid her sobs would wake up her sleeping husband. "Will the rest of our lives be like this—spent living in fear? Will you really allow them to harm us?"

Rosa tried to focus her mind on the many Bible verses that promised the Lord's protection. But then she thought about all the pastors who had been murdered. Fear pressed down upon her even more. "Please, Lord, help us to be strong!" she wept, feeling helpless and desperate.

Tired and burned out, she wondered if she should speak to José about leaving the country for a while. She wished they could live in a safe place for a few months, to recuperate from all the stress and worries they had faced during the last few years. With that wonderful wish flooding her heart with hope, at last she fell asleep.

Later on that night she told José how she felt. To her surprise, he agreed. "Yes, we do need a break," he said, "and we need it quickly. I think our lives are in serious danger."

"Rosa . . . children, go pack a bag," he said decisively the next morning. "Hurry, because we don't have much time." Each family member packed a suitcase, and then they left the house.

With the help of Christian brothers and sisters who understood the immense strain they had been under, the Ocaldos traveled abroad for some time to regain their strength. A church in another country provided a house and gave them all kinds of practical help.

Once in a safe place, they were finally able to unpack their bags. Since they had left in such a hurry, Rosa had not had time to supervise her girls as they packed. She could not help but smile as she looked inside Patricia's suitcase. It was full to the brim with all her dolls and stuffed animals.

For several months José, Rosa, and their two daughters were showered with love and fellowship. The family flourished during this time of rest and restoration.

Today, the Ocaldo family is back in Colombia, except for Adriana, who is continuing her studies abroad. José, Rosa, and Patricia are carrying on their ministry despite the ever-deteriorating political circumstances and the increasing violence in their homeland.

For safety reasons the family has moved to a different area far away from José's and Rosa's parents. This has made life difficult for Rosa, although in a different way than before. She often feels isolated and lonely. But she remains a soldier for Jesus.

I recently read a letter from Rosa, and it touched my heart. "The battle continues," she wrote, "but while our lives are constantly threatened, the church of Christ continues to win battles against Satan."

When we pray for the Suffering Church, it is important for us to remember that the battle isn't always overt and observable. Sometimes the warfare is spiritual and, therefore, invisible. But in either case Jesus has promised us ultimate victory. As the apostle John wrote long ago, "The one who is in you is greater than the one who is in the world" (1 John 4:4).

# SILVIA RUIZ

## A VERY STRONG WOMAN

During Johan's visit to Peru, he visited another prison—the Miguel Castro Castro Prison. There was a time of singing there, too, and the words "I have decided to follow Jesus" soared to the heavens.

C H A P T E R

We know that in all things God works for the good of those who love him, who have been called according to his purpose.

*Romans 8:28*

One of the Castro Castro inmates, Wuille Ruiz, was imprisoned under similar circumstances to those of Juan Carlos. Like Juan Carlos, Wuille was dragged away from his family and jailed on trumped-up charges, specifically that he had used his home for the purpose of spreading "subversive propaganda." Unlike Juan Carlos's wife, Pelagia, Silvia Ruiz was not arrested or jailed. But Silvia has seen her own share of pain and rejection, struggle and despair. Her story begins in February 1993, just days just after her husband's initial arrest.

Every time Silvia went to the local *Dincote* headquarters, where Wuille was first held, officials told her not to worry. "He'll be released soon," they assured her. She couldn't understand it. Despite their promises, day after day he remained behind bars. Why didn't somebody just send him home?

Silvia is a persistent woman. After a few days the guards grew weary of her queries, and their tone changed drastically. When Wuille's mother inquired about her son's well-being she got a different kind of answer. "Don't ask too many questions," an official warned, "otherwise your daughter-in-law might be arrested, too."

After Silvia heard this, her hopes began to plummet. With every passing day, she had less idea what to do or whom to believe.

At the same time, Wuille was being pressured to falsely confess to things he had not done. Whenever she was able to see him, Silvia was shocked at the sight of his strained face. Each time she watched him handcuffed and led away, the seriousness of their situation sank in further: Wuille was a prisoner. He was being held on false charges, he was probably being tortured, and there seemed to be no way to help him.

## A Twenty-Year Sentence

It soon became clear to the Ruizes that the authorities had allowed Silvia to visit Wuille in order to increase the pressure on him. "Do as we tell you," they cautioned him, "otherwise you may not see your family for a very long time." Eventually they made good on their threats. Silvia's visitation privileges were cut off. For her that simply meant that she had to find some other way to see her husband.

Silvia resorted to trying to talk to Wuille from the street. She realized that this could be dangerous, but she needed to hear his voice. Day after day, looking a little crazed, she ran along the street shouting his name through the air vents of the building where he was being held.

"Wuille Ruiz! Wuille Ruiz! Are you there?"

Silvia shouted until Wuille finally answered. For a while it was the only contact they had.

During those days Silvia's hopes for an early release withered. As her despair increased so did her sense of isolation. Wuille's former employers at CEDRO, the Center for the Prevention of Drug Use, offered their help. But everywhere else she turned for help she was rebuffed or ignored.

Unfortunately, this was true even at their church.

Silvia made an appointment with her pastor, hoping that Wuille's involvement as a youth leader and a member of the church board might help to clear his record. After a cool welcome into the pastor's office, Silvia listened in disbelief to his chilly words:

"I'm sorry, Silvia, but I can't provide you with any records of your husband's church involvement." The pastor refused to meet her eyes. "We cannot afford to put our fellowship in jeopardy. I'm sure you can understand our concerns."

Without question, the pastor's fear was legitimate. In 1993 no one dared talk openly about what was happening in Peru. It was common knowledge that innocent people like Wuille were arrested without reason and were often tortured by the *Dincote*. Putting oneself on the line on their behalf was futile—it only added to the numbers of those imprisoned.

Silvia refused to give up. As she searched her mind for new ways to seek Wuille's release, she became sadly aware of how differently she had once envisioned her life. She and Wuille had met while they were studying at the same university. After graduating from law school, Wuille had joined CEDRO, a prestigious, internationally recognized organization. His job was to support inmates who joined the drug rehabilitation program, and he had often visited the Castro Castro prison in that capacity.

Just before Wuille's arrest, Silvia had received a scholarship to finish her own master's degree in Community Development. But once he was locked up, her dreams of completing her degree were shattered. Their way of life seemed irretrievably lost.

It didn't take long for the financial burden of Wuille's absence to catch up with Silvia. For three months she lived on her husband's final salary. Then she used her scholarship money to provide for her daughter, Esteli, and herself. Finally, she had to move in with her parents because she could no longer afford the rent payment on her own small apartment. Buying food to take to Wuille was a great strain on her small budget, but it was the last thing she wanted to give up.

Silvia's attempts to deliver food to Wuille in the *Dincote* jail were both humiliating and frightening. For hours she had to stand in line, after which she was subject to a thorough body search. Even the food was checked. Her wrist was stamped in ink to seal the procedure. It would have been far easier to stop trying, but Silvia's love for her husband compelled her.

In August 1994, eighteen months after his arrest, Wuille's trial finally took place. Silvia wasn't permitted to enter the courtroom, so she and her sister-in-law anxiously waited outside. When they saw their lawyer emerge from the building, his grim expression told them everything they needed to know.

"Twenty years, Silvia," he said softly.

"*Twenty years?* You can't be serious. For what? What did he do to deserve twenty years?"

"I'm sorry." The attorney shook his head in disbelief. "Believe me, their minds were made up before I ever opened my mouth."

All of Silvia's bottled-up emotions exploded. She wept. She raged. Most of all, she felt utterly powerless. There was absolutely nothing she could do to help her husband.

After a few moments Silvia got herself under control. Under no circumstances did she want Wuille to see her so agitated and distressed. When he walked out of the courtroom on his way to the Castro Castro prison, she stood up straight and gave him a brave smile. The last thing she wanted to do was to add to his suffering.

Wuille's lawyer wasn't finished. A few months later he appealed Wuille Ruiz's sentence. But the authorities were unbending. In December 1994 the Supreme Court ratified Wuille's twenty-year sentence.

There was nothing more to be done except to pray, watch, and wait. By now Silvia was nearly overwhelmed with despair and anger. She was exhausted by the care of her very young child, the continuous financial strain, concern for her aging parents, endless worry about her husband. The list went on and on, and many times her situation was more than she could bear.

## A STRANGE SENSE OF BELONGING

Silvia's monthly visits to the prison were inevitably humiliating ordeals. She stood in line, no matter how hot or rainy or cold the weather, totally neglected by the prison guards. Women wearing rubber gloves sometimes appeared, randomly selecting visitors for intimate searches. Even though she never had to undergo that gruesome procedure, the very sight of the women with the gloves sent shivers down Silvia's spine.

Everything was done to prevent weapons and drugs from being smuggled into the prison, so even Esteli's diapers were checked. This worried Silvia—she didn't want her little girl accustomed to the touch of strangers. Was it wiser to leave the child at home rather than take her to see her father?

Everything Silvia did seemed to involve disturbing ethical considerations. As Esteli grew, Silvia tried to help her remember that she had a father. But taking her to the prison was more for Wuille's comfort, not Esteli's. Leaving a child that age at home would have been a relief for any mother, but it would have meant heartache to Wuille.

Ironically, the prison visits were the only occasions where Silvia felt a sense of belonging. As the wife of a prisoner, in society's eyes, she, too, was considered guilty of a crime. She was stigmatized nearly everywhere she went. But standing there, in line with the other women, she felt completely accepted by them.

As the months of Wuille's detention turned into years, Silvia's compassion for the other waiting women grew. She learned that many of them suffered even more that she did. At least she didn't have to travel for *days* to see her husband. She discovered that some of the prisoner's wives were not able to visit at all simply because they couldn't afford the journey. Silvia's conversations with women in line were often quite revealing.

"How do you manage to make ends meet financially?" Silvia asked one of the other women.

The woman took a drag on her cigarette and exhaled slowly. "Well, of course I haven't told my husband, but I've taken in a roommate."

"Oh, really? That's a good idea. Is her husband in prison too?"

"No, no," the woman laughed. "It's not a woman. It's a man I work with. He always liked me, even before the arrest. So it's a fair exchange. He gets what he wants, and I get some financial help."

As Esteli grew older, Silvia found it hard to know just exactly what to tell her about Wuille. Should she be told that he was a prisoner or not? Eventually Silvia decided to tell her daughter that Wuille was working at the place where they visited him and that he was just too busy to come home. Esteli accepted that, even though she was sometimes angry that her father's job required him to be away for so long.

Throughout the imprisonment, Silvia did what she could to create good family memories for Esteli. She was careful always to speak well of Wuille, and sometimes she had special surprises for the little girl.

"Look, Esteli! Your daddy bought you a birthday present!"

"How did he know it was my birthday? He's never here."

"Of course he knows it's your birthday, darling. He loves you very much. Let's see what he bought you."

Needless to say it was Silvia who bought the presents for Esteli's birthdays. And invariably she wondered afterwards if telling those "white lies" had been the right thing to do.

## IF ONLY WE HAD KNOWN . . .

By the time I heard Silvia's story for myself—I was privileged to have a long conversation with her not long after Wuille's release—I was convinced that we hadn't done enough for her and her family. Silvia's marriage to a man accused of terrorism had brought her into extreme poverty through no fault of her own. In order to feed her baby she'd sometimes had to go hungry herself. Though she was an educated woman, she was unable to find steady employment because no one would hire a "terrorist's" wife.

*If only we had known . . .* , I thought to myself as Silvia shared her experiences with me.

Finances were disastrous. Child rearing was a continuous challenge. But there was more—Silvia's relationship with Wuille was stretched to the maximum, too. One day after the Supreme Court ratified his sentence, Wuille became very emotional during a visit.

"Silvia," he said, his voice breaking, "I want you to know that I would understand if you filed for a divorce. In fact, that might be the best option for you. I can't ask you to wait twenty years for me. You need to get on with your life."

Silvia was stunned and angry. "You should know me better than that!"

"Don't be upset, Silvia. I'm thinking of you, not of myself."

"Do you think I'd want you to divorce me if I were in prison? How dare you suggest such a thing to me? I can't believe it would

even cross your mind that I would file for divorce under these circumstances!"

Silvia remained faithful. She worked job after job. Bright as
she was, nothing was too menial for her. She cleaned houses. She
did data entry. She worked as a secretary. She took any job she could
find.

To avoid the social problems that came with being a prisoner's
wife, she decided to allow her coworkers to assume that she and her
husband were separated. It was a safe way to prevent unwelcome
questions. And it certainly was true, wasn't it?

Of course Silvia wasn't the only one who felt the pain of
Wuille's imprisonment. His mother was devastated by what happened to him, and her first—and last—prison visit turned out to be
more than she could bear. She was in poor health to begin with even
before he was arrested. She suffered from arthritis and was hardly
able to walk.

All his life Wuille had been a perfect son—her youngest—and
the apple of his mother's eye. She could hardly bear the sight of him
in his prison garb, looking so weary and gaunt. But the worst blow
came when she begged the guards for one small favor.

"Could I please hold my son's hand? I just want to touch him,
even if it's just for a minute."

"It's against regulations," the guard growled.

"But he's my son. . . ." The old woman began to weep.

"I said, it's *against regulations!* Don't ask me again."

Not long after the visit, Wuille's mother died.

"I just couldn't find the words to tell Wuille the sad news,"
Silvia told me. "When I went to see him, I tried to avoid the subject.
I mechanically answered his questions, but Wuille sensed that
something was wrong.

"What is it, Silvia? There's something you're not telling me."

"What do you mean?"

"I mean I know you very well. Something has happened, and
you're afraid to tell me. Is it my mother? Is she ill?"

"Oh, Wuille . . ."

"She's gone, isn't she?"

When Silvia finally told him the whole story, she learned that
God had prepared Wuille's heart to receive the sad news. The Lord

gave him a dream in which his mother was leaving him. The dream caused him to write a "life letter," which he asked Silvia to read at the funeral.

Meanwhile, Silvia's mother had been sick, too, suffering from tuberculosis. In their precarious financial straits, the family didn't have enough money to buy the proper medicine for her, so her health deteriorated. The care and worry for Silvia and Esteli also aggravated her physical problems. One night Silvia heard a scream from the bathroom.

"Silvia! Come and help me!"

Silvia rushed to her mother's side. She got there just in time to prevent her from falling. Later that evening the frail old woman died in Silvia's arms.

"A tremendous feeling of guilt flooded my heart," Silvia told me, recalling the days after her mother's death. "I had felt torn between my child, my husband, and my mother. I knew my mother was ill, but I was so busy taking care of Wuille and Esteli that I just couldn't find the time and energy to look after her properly. I neglected her, but it was too late to do something about that—she was gone."

## Soul-Searching Questions

In hindsight Silvia told me that, even with the remorse she experienced, she felt the death of her mother had a positive effect on her. "My mother was a very strong woman. Now that I was no longer able to lean on her shoulder, I felt my own strength increase. It was almost as if I became more and more like my mother as time passed."

All the death and disappointment took their toll on Silvia. For the first time since his arrest, she began to feel anger toward Wuille. This stirred up an enormous wrestling match between her mind and her emotions. Her mind told her that Wuille was not to be blamed—it was not his fault that he was in prison. Yet her emotions continually reminded her that if Wuille had been home, she could have been a better daughter. She could have bought the medicines her mother needed.

"Gradually," Silvia told me, "I began to realize that it might be time to alter my priorities. For three years Wuille had been at the top of my list. My whole life had centered around him—advocating his case, providing his food, visiting him—it had cost me so much time and energy."

*Maybe it's time to put Esteli first,* Silvia told herself.

And that raised yet another question. *Where do I fit in?* Silvia began to wonder. Did her needs matter at all? Where was her identity? Did she live only to care for others?

"I had wanted so much to finish my education, but despite all my years of hard work at the university, look at the jobs I was doing. Now that my mother was gone, as the oldest daughter, I was the matriarch of the family as well. Wasn't it time to start thinking about myself?"

It was difficult for Silvia to express these feelings to me. She thought they sounded shallow and selfish. I tried to help her understand that these were legitimate questions that many women in different corners of the world have asked themselves at one time or another. They were also questions that only God could answer.

Even in the midst of this emotional turmoil, Wuille's letters from prison were a great source of comfort to Silvia. In carefully worded pages that sounded a little like epistles, he encouraged his wife to be patient and to continue trusting in the Lord. Although her thoughts about him were not always positive, Silvia was strengthened by the assurance of his love for her and Esteli. She knew she had married a good husband.

Looking back, Silvia feels the third year of Wuille's imprisonment was the hardest. But it was also the year God opened a new door for her. She met a lawyer who told her about a group called *Paz y Esperanza,* Peace and Hope. This legal organization advocated the cases of Christians who were unjustly imprisoned. Perhaps they could find ways to help Wuille Ruiz.

Open Doors was in close contact with this group, and that's how we first learned about the Ruiz family's predicament. Through our magazines and prayer ministry, we did what we could to ask people to pray for Wuille and Silvia. Before long, the Ruizes began to receive letters and cards of encouragement from all over the world, marking the end of their isolation. Pastors and churches in Peru also began to extend helping hands.

Then Silvia began to help out in the office of *Paz y Esperanza.* "Contributing to the needs of others caused a huge change in me." Silvia's face brightened as she approached the end of her story. "To my surprise, I noticed that I was beginning to be more patient. I could better cope with my situation. I began to accept the court's verdict and put Esteli first.

"At night, when the business of the day had passed and I had time to think, I would often take out the pile of letters and cards I had received. Reading the hopeful words, especially the ones little children wrote to Esteli and me, lifted my spirits and helped me to cast all my cares upon the Lord."

After more than five years in prison, and quite unexpectedly, Wuille was released. The evening before, at a large Christian gathering in Lima, the attendees had spent special time in prayer for the Ruiz family, asking the Lord to release Wuille. Contrary to custom, on the next day, a Saturday, President Fujimori of Peru went to his office and signed the decree that secured Wuille's release under the Law of Pardon.

When she heard the good news, Silvia was both elated and shocked at the same time. It was wonderful that Wuille was coming home, but where in the world was she going to put him? Her parent's small house, which she and Esteli were sharing with her father and sister, only had two bedrooms. She couldn't very well ask her father and sister to leave their own house, so the only place for Wuille was the sofa in the living room.

## HELP AND HEALING

The day Silvia and I talked, it had been five months since her happy reunion with Wuille. Life was still not easy. They longed for the privacy of their own home, a quiet place where they could be together and just catch up. Wuille, like many other released prisoners, had become accustomed to extreme quiet. The ordinary noises of an active household were difficult for him to tolerate.

In the meantime lots of effort was expended filling out the

necessary paperwork to get Wuille's record cleared. Under the Law of Pardon, prisoners are released, but they continue to have a criminal record. Wuille had finished his education in law, but in order to be certified as a lawyer, he was told that it would cost him about $3,000 to clear his record. It was an impossible amount of money for Wuille and Silvia to earn.

By God's grace, they were spared the challenge of raising the money. On November 24, 1998, a law was passed in Peru that cleared the criminal record of those falsely convicted of terrorism. This law benefited all the evangelicals who suffered years of unjust imprisonment.

Even more recently, Christian friends have made it possible for Wuille and Silvia to rent a small apartment of their own. At long last they are able to enjoy some privacy.

The Ruiz family's struggles are still not over. They need our continued prayers for healing and direction. But in spite of everything, Silvia and Wuille are still following Jesus. Wuille has grown in his faith, and Silvia has become a very strong woman in her own right. We can only guess how God will use them in the future, but one thing is certain—they are promised that "in all things God works for the good of those who love him, who have been called according to his purpose."

Silvia and Wuille love God. He has called them. And come what may, whatever he has promised—to them, to you, and to me—he will surely accomplish.

# EUROPE

# ESTHER AND KHAMIRA

## TWO WOMEN, BOUND TOGETHER

One look at a few photographs of Grozny, Chechnya, would convince most of us that the worst has already happened there; that there's really nothing anyone can do for that place. Shelled out buildings. Mortar holes. Eerie, silent streets. Not only has the city been utterly demolished by war, but it continues to be devastated by anarchy and corruption. It is a place of little beauty and even less hope.

CHAPTER 19

Chechnya was invaded by Russia in 1994. The Chechen people, enraged by the invasion, fought desperately for their independence. The war's carnage was outrageous, and the destruction was incomparable. Over the course of eighteen months, it is estimated that 2 million bombs were

Wake up! Strengthen what remains and is about to die.

*Revelation 3:2*

dropped on Grozny, leaving virtually every building in ruins. In the midst of this calamity, many of the ethnic Russians fled, along with countless others of various ethnicities.

Those who survived and did not flee were mostly old, infirm, or helpless. They found themselves living in a ghost town of shelled-out structures with no electricity, no heat, no running water, and no food. When relief organizations sent in basic supplies, enterprising criminals stole and sold the donated necessities meant to be given away.

## "YOU ARE A HERO!"

Into this scene of chaos and calamity walked a woman who is one of my personal heroines. "Esther" had a heart for the Suffering Church, traveling to the most dangerous and deserted places on the European continent to bring help and encouragement. She sought out beleaguered believers doing their best to serve the Lord under the worst possible circumstances, and she helped them in the most creative and visionary ways imaginable.

Two years after the end of the war, Esther went to Grozny. She put on an old dress, tied a scarf around her head, and crossed the border into a nightmare. Once she got off the bus and looked around, Esther could hardly believe her eyes. Not one building was intact, and there were no signs of reconstruction or repair. Because the war to gain independence from Russia had been lost, all the destruction and suffering had been in vain. Survivors were left dispirited and without purpose.

Yet people still lived in Grozny. In the midst of the rubble, Esther was introduced to Christians who were faithfully trusting the Lord to come to their aid. Some were at the point of death. Others limped along without help, possessing little more than faith. One of these courageous Chechens was a woman named "Khamira," whom Esther had met on an earlier trip.

"Sister, you are a heroine!" Khamira hugged Esther warmly. "Nobody dares to come here anymore, and yet you've come to see us. You really are a heroine!"

Tears streamed down Khamira's deeply lined face as all the hurt and pain she'd experienced found its way out. It had been months since she'd met a visitor from abroad. She had felt so isolated and deserted. And now Esther had come.

Esther hardly saw herself as a heroine, but she was thankful her visit was bringing encouragement. She would have preferred to spend that long Pentecost weekend in Holland with her family. After weeks of rain the sun had just started to shine on the Dutch countryside a few days before she'd left. But Esther had been informed that an appointment had been set up for her with a government official. She had been trying for some time to secure official permission to take Christian literature into Chechnya, and this might be her only chance.

"How in the world did you manage to get here?" Khamira wanted to know. "Don't you realize that you could be kidnapped or killed? More than one hundred people have been abducted here. President Yeltsin sent his official representative to negotiate, and within an hour of his arrival in Chechnya even he was kidnapped!"

"Well, it's not so bad for me," Esther explained with a grin. "I'm not a political person."

"That doesn't mean you're safe! All the organizations that used to work here have left: the Red Cross, Médicins Sans Frontières, Dorcas Aid, and World Vision. Yet you came! It's amazing!"

"Well, it certainly was a long trip, and at times it was pretty hazardous, but I made it through. The Lord must have a purpose in my being here." Esther smiled. It had been a long and hazardous trip indeed. It had been unreal and certainly unsafe. In fact, the more she thought about it, the more Esther was amazed by the deep peace she felt throughout the journey.

*If I'd realized the danger involved*, she thought to herself, *I might have thought twice about it.*

## JOURNEY INTO ANARCHY

After flying from Amsterdam to Moscow and then from Moscow farther south on a domestic flight, she and a local colleague had driven to the city of Nalchik in Balkaria, then on to Vladikavkaz in the Caucasus range. There they were briefed on how to get safely into Chechnya. A young Russian couple, refugees from Chechnya, and an old lady had then boarded a bus with them.

"Ah, so you traveled with Sasha, Natasha, and Olga," Khamira beamed. "They are so dear to us. They keep bringing us food and goods from Vladikavkaz. I don't know how we would survive without them!"

"They're brave, all right," Esther agreed. Then she filled Khamira in on some of the details of their journey. They were constantly checked and rechecked at the several roadblocks they encountered, but to Esther's surprise, nobody asked her any questions. She was dressed like the other women, and she'd kept very quiet, which may have helped—and, of course, she was praying continuously.

The last part of their journey was traveled by minibus. All the bus windows had been blacked out and covered with tape. As soon as they pulled out of the bus station, two male passengers unzipped their duffel bags and pulled out automatic rifles, which they kept close at hand—just in case.

Needless to say, the atmosphere inside the bus was incredibly tense. "This is the region where most of the shootings and abductions take place," one of Esther's companions whispered. "It's no-man's-land."

The driver was afraid, too, and the bus hurtled along the poorly maintained roadway at breakneck speed. Esther simply closed her eyes and prayed, trying to ignore her fear.

Thank God that part of the trip was behind her! And now there were more important things at hand. "How are you, Khamira? And how is the church?"

While Khamira poured tea for her visitor, more and more women found their way into the bombed-out apartment where Esther and Khamira were talking. News had quickly spread that a visitor from abroad had come. Starving for encouragement, everyone wanted to come and greet Esther.

"Life has not been easy here," Khamira said sadly. "Since the war, many of the Russian families from our church have left. They've settled in Stavropol province, in a village with no gas, water, or electricity. But at least they are safe. I certainly don't blame them for leaving. The war was so terrible. In a year and a half, 10 percent of our population was killed—125,000 people lost their lives."

"It must be very difficult for you to find the most basic supplies," Esther remarked, glancing around the poorly furnished apartment.

"Yes, it's nearly impossible. We have a shortage of everything—food, medicine, clothing, bedding. And now that the humanitarian aid organizations have left, the situation can only get worse. The leaders of our Baptist denomination don't visit us any more—it's too dangerous for them to come to Chechnya. They're afraid they'll be kidnapped. And all of us are constantly being pressured to move to Russia."

"Wouldn't that make life a little easier for you? Why are you so determined to stay?"

"Because the good news is that Muslims are very open toward the gospel here, Esther. At least twenty have come to Christ recently. What will happen to them if we all leave? We feel we have a ministry in this place."

Esther could hardly believe her ears. In 1989 the first mosque was opened in Chechnya. Now there were a total of 637 mosques in the country. Islamization was moving fast, and Wahhabism, a puritanical form of Islam, was widespread in the area, receiving strong support from Saudi Arabia. Yet, even there, in that extreme Muslim country, where it was nearly impossible to survive as a Christian and the political situation was a powder keg, God still had his people—people with vision to reach the lost.

"How can you evangelize when the Muslims are so militant?" Esther asked Khamira. "One official told me that he's afraid Chechnya will turn into another Afghanistan, with a Taliban-like movement and a civil war."

Khamira nodded. "It isn't easy, of course, and we have no idea what tomorrow holds."

"How many evangelical Christians are left here?"

"I think there are only about two hundred now," Khamira answered. "There is the Baptist church, where we go, and an Adventist church. There is also a secret group of believers from Muslim backgrounds. About two-thirds of the Christians in our church are women, and most of them are widows. Many of our husbands and sons were killed during the war."

At this point Khamira stopped talking. Her eyes misted over, and Esther remembered that her husband had been killed by sniper fire during one of the attacks on the city. As she had no children, Khamira was all alone.

"No, we're not thinking of leaving," Khamira insisted, and the other women nodded in agreement. "Where would we go? Besides, we have work to do here. Our neighbors need us. We have so many opportunities to share the love of Christ with others."

"You say there are mostly widows left behind. What about children? Are there war orphans in Grozny?"

Khamira nodded her head sadly. "Oh yes, there are many orphaned children. And their need breaks my heart! Many are in terrible physical condition and are suffering emotionally because of the trauma they've seen. Chechen and Russian children suffer equally. I so wish we could do something for them."

"I wish we could do something for the children, too," Esther agreed. *And I know exactly what I'd like to do,* she added silently.

As she looked around the city in the days that followed and saw its poverty and hopelessness, she felt grieved that she had nothing practical to offer. *I should have brought suitcases full of supplies!* she scolded herself. *If only I had known. . . .*

## A WINDOW OF OPPORTUNITY

As it turned out, Esther's appointment with the government official was very productive. Although he was a Muslim in that stressful area, he seemed to be a reasonable, moderate man. "Would you like for me to take you on a tour of Grozny? You can see the churches for yourself."

"That would be very interesting," Esther said. The next thing she knew, bodyguards with their automatic weapons were following every step she and her companions took, their guns at the ready. First they visited the Orthodox church building. It was in complete ruins. Then they went to the Baptist church and the Adventist church.

"These buildings seem to have been hardly hit," Esther commented.

"I know," their Muslim host answered heartily. "Let me tell you why. God is righteous. Throughout the war with Russia, I have seen with my own eyes who the real Christians are—who the real people of the Book are."

He went on to explain how the Russian Orthodox patriarch had blessed the tanks and the soldiers who came to kill the Chechen people. "You've seen what is left of the Orthodox church," the man chuckled. "On the other hand, the Baptist Christians continued to live in their house of prayer, and during the war they never skipped a Sunday service. They prayed day and night and shared what they had with the Chechens. The fact that their buildings remain unscathed is a miracle from God.

"It is my personal opinion that if anything stopped that terrible war, it wasn't an act of politicians or pressure from the West. It was only because of the prayers of these believers."

When it was time to talk business, Esther knew she needed to make use of the opportunity that had been presented to her. She felt the Lord had given her favor with this official, and it was the time to act. No one knew how long the door to this country would be open for Bibles to be brought in. With radical Muslims in power, it might well be impossible to import any literature for the next ten years. Esther asked permission to bring in a large amount of Scriptures—Bibles, New Testaments, and children's Bibles. Even though there were not many Christians left in the country, Muslims were finding Christ, and they needed the Word of God to grow in their faith.

"There is more," Esther added. "It would be so wonderful if a special retreat could be held for the Christians from Chechnya where they could receive pastoral care. It would be a time when they could laugh and cry together. Could you look into giving us permission for that as well?"

Last but not least, Esther wanted something for those war-torn boys and girls. "Would you also be willing to grant us permission to organize three summer camps for children?"

The government official stared at the brave woman for a few moments. He seemed to be silently counting the cost of all her requests. Finally, after a lengthy pause, he spoke. "Frankly, I'm happy to find a Christian organization willing to take all these risks. I appreciate the courage you've shown by coming here. On behalf of the government of Chechnya I grant you the three requests, provided you take the necessary precautions to ensure the safety of all involved."

As they worked out further details, Esther could hardly contain her joy.

With a heart overflowing with thankfulness, Esther went to say good-bye to Khamira. Now, at last, she had something to offer. Something more than her presence. Something more than words.

"Khamira! Guess what!" Esther exclaimed as soon as she arrived at the woman's door. "Remember what you told me about the children? Well, we have permission to organize three summer camps. We will be able to also supply you with Bibles and children's Bibles before too long. The Lord has answered our prayers—you and the other Christians will be able to go to a Christian retreat!"

As they hugged and said good-bye, Esther and Khamira were both crying. Here were two women living in different countries under different circumstances. But one thing bound them together—both of them were part of the body of Christ.

## A Smoldering Wick

Esther's plans were fulfilled, and her goals were accomplished. The children's camps and adult retreats took place as planned, and the Bibles were safely delivered. In the weeks and months that followed, however, the situation in Grozny deteriorated even more.

When I saw Esther after a later trip to Chechnya, she was uncharacteristically grim. "Oh, Anneke, what I have seen and heard about Chechnya has really shaken me."

She went on to tell me what had happened. In October 1998 the Baptist pastor, Alexei Sitnikov, was kidnapped, tortured, and killed. Deacon Alexander Kulakov, a godly man who stepped into Pastor Alexei's role, preached against corruption one Sunday morning. The next week he, too, disappeared, and a church member soon made a grisly discovery at the marketplace—he found Kulakov's severed head on display. Middle-aged and elderly women were unable to go out of their homes because the danger of rape was so great. The Muslim government official who helped Esther was murdered as well.

Because of the increasing violence and anarchy, many Christians in Grozny—including Khamira—finally agreed to leave. They were evacuated to Krasnodar, in Russia, where a "house of refuge" was bought for them. During the latest Russian bombardments, the majority of the Chechen population fled abroad. Some Christians moved to the refugee camps in neighboring Ossetia.

Sometimes it seems as if God has moved the lampstand from its place (Revelation 2:5). But God promises in Isaiah 42:3 that "a bruised reed he will not break, and a smoldering wick he will not snuff out." Women like Khamira are regaining health and strength in their new homes, filling their houses with song as they go about their daily duties. And Esther? She continues her ministry in the area. By word and deed the love of Christ is shared in the refugee camps. The small group of Christians there may be a smoldering wick—but definitely not snuffed out!

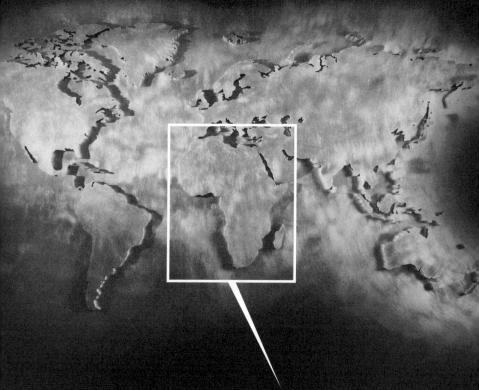

AFRICA

# AMAL

## IN THE HANDS OF JESUS

Through the bars that crossed the windows in her mud-brick house, Amal looked up at the sky. It was impossible to count the stars; there were too many of them. Although it was midnight, it was hot, and she was having trouble falling asleep. As she looked at her husband sleeping soundly beside her, she quietly whispered a prayer for his health and thanked the Lord for the many blessings their family had received.

## CHAPTER 20

Suddenly the silence of the night was broken by a car screeching to a halt in front of their compound. Amal sat bolt upright in bed to listen. Doors slammed, and she heard voices she didn't recognize. Then there was a firm knock at the gate.

"Open up!" the voice shouted. Amal leaped to her feet in alarm.

> The Lord is my light and my salvation—whom shall I fear? The Lord is the stronghold of my life—of whom shall I be afraid?
>
> *Psalm 27:1*

Squinting into the darkness, she saw two men and a car. "Is this Ali's house?" a heavily armed officer asked.

"Yes," Amal answered, surprised at herself for feeling so calm. "Please come in."

Ali was awake by now and standing outside their sleeping quarters. "I'm the one you are looking for," he said. "What is the problem?"

"We have orders to take you to the police station," the man answered.

"Then I would like to pray with my family before I come with you."

The commotion had awakened all six of the children. They were trembling with fear, but joining hands with their parents, they quietly formed a circle. Their father's firm, confident voice was full of faith as he committed the whole family into the hands of their heavenly Father. Afterwards, he hugged each of them good-bye and left with the policemen.

## A NIGHT TO REMEMBER

As the car drove away into the night, Amal knew very well that she might be in for a difficult time. But she was prepared. Ali's family had threatened to kill him, and she and Ali had often discussed the possibility of those threats being fulfilled. His family knew that they were entitled by law to kill anyone who left the Islamic faith. That was exactly what Amal and Ali had done.

The couple had long been aware that it would only take a distant relative's report to the authorities for the wheels of capital punishment to start turning. Even now, with Ali taken from her and the future left in complete uncertainty, Amal felt no remorse about any aspect of their decision. How *could* she, after all God had done for them?

No, there were no regrets, but the sadness they all felt was profound. The children cried quietly. One of the older boys said, "Mother, what can we do? How can we help him?"

Amal put her arm around her son. "There's really nothing we can do for him now but pray."

All of them returned to bed without a word. Amal determined that at first light she would try to find out where Ali had been taken and what the authorities intended to do with him. But sleep did not return to her that night. As she lay tossing and turning, her thoughts replayed a series of events from the past.

She remembered the mountainous area where she and Ali had grown up. Unlike the desert where they now lived, the landscape of their childhood was green and lush. Amal loved the beauty of the trees and shrubbery that adorned the surroundings of her early years. Life was uncomplicated in those days.

Amal was very young when she met Ali. His friendliness and his zeal for Allah attracted her. At school he was a diligent student of the Koran, and his teachers noted that he would make a wonderful teacher. So that's what Ali was trained to be—an Imam—a teacher of Islam.

Soon after Amal married Ali, a door opened for them to go to Oman, one of the Gulf States. For five years Ali taught the precepts of Islam to the wealthy people there and led prayers in the mosque. He very convincingly warned his audiences about the dangers of other faiths.

"Islam is the only true religion, and the Bible is a dangerous book," he repeatedly told the faithful Muslims. "The Bible has been changed many times throughout the centuries, and it is not true. Don't read it!"

A smile formed on Amal's face as she remembered the birth of their children. Ali had been such a proud father. In seven years time, six children were added to the family. Their twin boys arrived first, then two more boys came, one right after the other. Two daughters made their family complete.

The family had prospered in Oman. Life there was very different from the first years of their marriage when they were still living in their African homeland. In Oman it was not difficult to live comfortably. Ali's position in the mosque gave him status and money to provide well for his wife and children. They had even managed to save enough to buy some land after they returned to their homeland.

*The Lord knew we would need this place,* Amal reflected as she lay awake in the dark. Upon their return from Oman, they had bought a small lot on the outskirts of the capital city. The building materials consisted of sand, water, and straw. Their home was fenced off by a mud wall, and the children were able to play in the small courtyard between the rooms. It was nothing fancy, but Ali and Amal were grateful for a place to call their own.

Then, in 1995 their quiet lives changed completely. It all had started the year before when one of Ali's friends, a Muslim from his youth, gave him a Bible. "This book changed my life," he told Ali. "You should read it, too."

"You know what I think about this book," Ali had responded.

"I know, I know. Just take a look at it anyway."

For some reason Ali secretly followed the advice of his friend. At first Amal couldn't believe her eyes when she saw him reading it.

She decided to remain quiet and not stir up a fuss. Then, gradually, Ali began to confide in her.

"Amal, this is very interesting. It's so unlike the Koran. I'm learning so much about Jesus."

"Aren't you being a little bit hypocritical, reading that book after preaching against it for so many years?"

"It is never wrong to learn," he replied gently. Ali was obviously touched by what he was reading, and after several months, he called the family together.

## A LIFE AND DEATH DECISION

"I am not going to the mosque this morning," he announced one day in December 1995. "Some of you know that I've been studying the Bible. I have come to the conclusion that what is written there is true, and I've made a decision. From now on I am not just a believer but also a follower of Jesus Christ. I am going to the evangelical church this morning, and I will inform the pastor and the Christians there of my faith."

Amal had stared at Ali in disbelief. She would never forget the day—she had felt both frightened and proud at the same time. Amal always deeply respected her husband's judgment. She knew that he was sincere and that he would not do such a thing without the most serious consideration. He was both a thinker and an honest man. She also knew that Ali could never go against his own conscience. Amal could only hope that he would spell out for her the new truth he had found. Then she would decide for herself what to do.

That evening Ali gathered his wife and children around him. Clearly and convincingly he explained to them the basic truths of the Christian gospel.

"All of us have sinned," he told them. "Every person on earth has fallen short of the glory of God. That's why God sent his only Son, Jesus—both human and divine at the same time and without sin, to die for the sins of the whole world. All who believe that God sent Jesus and accept the sacrifice of Jesus on the cross will be saved and have eternal life."

The way Ali explained it sounded so simple and so true. Amal didn't need much time to decide. When Ali finished his clarification of the Good News, she and the children immediately accepted Jesus into their lives. They would follow Jesus as a family.

Of course, Ali's decision brought great encouragement to the pastor and the other Christians at the nearby church. They knew that such decisions were not made lightly—the repercussions of a Muslim coming to Christ would be far-reaching. When God revealed himself to a Muslim leader like Ali and did a work of grace in his heart, it was a demonstration of God's power to all of them.

Ali did not keep secret the change that had taken place in his life, and it wasn't long before word got out that he had become a Christian. He visited friends and relatives and told them openly about Christ. Of course they had already noticed that he didn't go to the mosque anymore.

One day when the pastor was visiting Ali's family, a relative arrived. From the look on his face, Amal could tell immediately that he didn't have friendly intentions.

"Ali," he started as soon as he had greeted everyone present, "is it true what I have heard? Have you become a *Kafir?* I'm told you don't go to the mosque anymore."

"It's true, my brother," Ali replied gently. "I have come to believe that Jesus Christ is the Way, the Truth, and the Life, and that he died for my sins. I know this upsets you, but I can't renounce my Savior."

The relative's face darkened. "You know that according to the Koran, I am entitled to kill you, don't you?" he threatened. "I can't believe that you, who once taught us—you, who know the Koran better than any of us—would believe in this nonsense. You have a choice, Ali. Return to Islam, or we will cut off your head!"

Ali was not intimidated. He just shrugged his shoulders. He had already counted the cost before publicly confessing his faith in Christ. "I'm not afraid," he replied. "Life on earth is short anyway, and I know where I'll go after I die."

The relative realized that further conversation was futile. There was no point in arguing with Ali. He turned his back on them and left the house in frustration.

The pastor, who had witnessed the incident, shook his head sadly. "You are now in the hands of Jesus, Ali."

Other family members also began to visit Amal and Ali's house, but they arrived with different intentions. They wanted to hear more about Jesus. The change in Ali and Amal's life and their enthusiasm about their newfound faith attracted a surprising number of friends and relatives. It wasn't long before they, too, had accepted Jesus. And their decision brought about severe consequences.

Ali's sister was sent away by her Muslim husband. Considered outcasts in their communities because they had become Christians, Ali's mother, his brother, his sister, and others in his immediate family took refuge on Ali's property. Several more huts were built inside their wall, making the little courtyard in the center smaller and smaller.

Ali had lost his job as a teacher in the mosque, but his church provided him with a job as technical inspector for church schools. Ali's new occupation took him to many cities and villages in the northern part of his country. Everywhere he went, he shared his newfound faith in Christ. Sharing the Good News with Muslims became the focal point of his life.

"If only you knew what is written in the Bible," he told them.

"Will you tell us?" they'd often reply.

And Ali would once again share the gospel with them.

Believing in Jesus had consequences for Ali and Amal's children. To begin with, they had to change schools—their parents certainly didn't want them to go to the Islamic public school anymore. So they went to a school run by the church where Ali and Amal now attended. The church school was farther away, so the children all left together every morning in a donkey cart. After the donkey died they had to make their way to school on the crowded, shabby, public transport bus.

Once they got home late in the afternoon, the children had plenty of chores to do. Since there was no running water, they had to take turns carrying water home from a communal pump. There they would meet the neighbor's children, also sent to get water for their mothers.

One day at the pump an argument arose. "I was here first," Amal's son Toufic insisted as he pushed away his friend.

"You're lying! I got here first," the neighbor kid countered. After more pushing and shoving, the fighting became serious.

All sorts of insults were exchanged, and one of the local boys said, "You've got no right to use this water at all—you and your family are *Kafirs.* You've betrayed the prophet!"

Toufic lost control and shouted, "You are a Muslim, and your prophet is dead. My prophet is alive and up in heaven, so you can't compare them. Muhammad is dead, but Jesus is alive!"

That was not a wise thing to say, but then children don't always think before they speak. In any case, the neighbors overheard the children, and word of the incident spread quickly throughout the community.

That had happened just a few days before. Now Ali had been taken by the security police. Was it because of Toufic's remarks? Or was it because one of their relatives had reported Ali's conversion in hopes that the government would condemn him to death?

*We may never know,* Amal sighed as she closed her eyes and tried to get a little sleep.

## FAITH BEHIND BARS

In the days that followed, Amal learned that Ali had been taken to a prison not too far away. It took her forty-five minutes by bus to get there. The daily trip was quite an ordeal because of the heat and the bumpy road, but Amal was thankful that she was allowed to take food to her husband. *At least he won't starve,* she told herself.

Prisoners were only allowed a small ration of beans and grit per day. In a corner of the prison, on a metal sheet with some burning wood underneath, each of them had to make his own portion of flat bread. Like some of the other prisoners' wives, Amal decided that she would make sure her husband's poor health wouldn't deteriorate further because of a lack of food and vitamins. Whatever happened, she would do what she could to look after him.

After Amal arrived, she was required to sit in a waiting room while a guard went to look for Ali in one of the prison compartments. Fortunately, he was not in isolation but could freely move around inside the prison. That gave him opportunity to talk to his fellow inmates. Once he was brought so see Amal, Ali's good mood invariably surprised her.

"How long do you think they can keep you here?" Amal asked him one day. Conversion from Islam had been a capital offense in their country for seven years. Amal knew that Ali had been accused of changing his religion and being absent from the mosque for more than two years. She had been present every time Ali had been brought into court, but the judge had always found an excuse not to pass sentence.

"I think the government is afraid to sentence me," Ali answered. "They're afraid it will give them an even worse reputation in the Western world if they put me to death because my case has been publicized abroad. But they can't let me go free either, because then the fundamentalist Muslims, including some of our own family members, would protest. And they have the law on their side; you know that, Amal."

"I know," Amal whispered. "But I'm worried about your health, Ali!"

Even before his arrest, Ali had suffered from chronic heart problems. "You've been in this unhealthy prison for over three months now," she complained one afternoon. "I was so glad when the judge finally agreed to transfer you to a hospital last week, but why are you still here? Why doesn't the prison do what the judge told them to do?"

"I don't know, Amal," Ali sighed, "but we have to keep trusting the Lord. You wouldn't want me to recant, Amal, would you?" Ali asked, looking into the beautiful brown eyes of his wife.

"No, Ali. Never!" The prosecutor had given him two months to recant and return to Islam. For Ali and Amal, freedom was simply not that precious.

"Amal, I need to talk to you," Ali's lawyer told her one day when they met at the prison. "I've had word that they are willing to let your husband go."

"Even without recanting?" Amal was surprised.

"Yes, but I want to warn you that I feel this is a trap. I've advised Ali to stay in prison because setting him free may be a backhanded way of getting rid of him. I think if he agrees to go home, his life will be in grave danger."

As much as Amal longed for Ali to be released, she trusted their lawyer. And Ali had already agreed to heed his advice. They both concurred that it was probably wise counsel.

Several days later, well after dark, there was a knock on Amal's gate.

When she opened it, two tall masked men forced themselves in.

"Where is Ali?" they demanded, their eyes darting around furtively.

"He's still in prison," Amal answered truthfully, her pulse racing.

"You are lying, woman!" one man said, shoving her aside. Amal noticed that he spoke with a thick accent. Without a word of explanation, they ransacked the family's small living quarters. It was quite a job since it was dark and the house had no electricity. With flashlights they searched for Ali hut by hut, but they didn't find him.

"We were told that he was released. Where is he?"

Amal and the children stood and watched with all the dignity they could muster. They were frightened but grateful. By God's grace, Ali was still in prison, and the men had to leave without him. Soon after the incident, Amal found out that the intruders belonged to an Iranian hit squad. They had orders to kill Ali.

## A WARM AFRICAN WELCOME

Ten months after Ali was imprisoned, I was given the opportunity to visit Amal. I wouldn't have missed it for anything. As our Jeep zigzagged to avoid the potholes on the sandy road, my adrenaline rose. This was the moment I had looked forward to since our plane took off from Schiphol airport in Amsterdam.

I now found myself in the front seat of a car with two local Christian men. Despite my head covering, it was still quite obvious that I was a foreigner, but Amal had insisted I visit her at home anyway. She had heard rumors that security police watched her house, but she didn't mind, and neither did I.

I knocked at the same gate where less than a year before the policemen had arrived to arrest Ali. But I received a very different welcome. Amal and her children were eagerly awaiting my visit. In the shade of one of the small huts on her compound, Amal had placed a table, some chairs, and a few benches.

Her dignified appearance amazed me. She had stylishly wrapped her head and body in a colorful *tob*—a five-yard-long piece of sky blue fabric. To my surprise I noticed that her toenails were neatly painted bright red. How important that splash of color was. The pressures of the life Amal endured could so easily have made her forget that she was a woman. It was obvious from the start that Amal faced the challenges of life head-on.

Even though her house was made of mud, the dirt floor had been carefully swept. I immediately noticed three trees in the yard—a well-trimmed guava tree, an orange tree, and a lemon tree—all flourishing. What a difference their green leaves made against the drab backdrop of light brown earth. On the way to Amal's house, we had seen nothing but sand and mud-brick houses for miles.

The children were all at home, well-dressed and clean. One by one they came to shake hands with me. Other relatives were there, too. As I looked into the wrinkled face of Ali's mother, I wondered what was going through her mind. She had found Jesus in her old age, and despite the fact that her son was taken away from her, she seemed content.

"Thank you for coming." Amal smiled at me when we all sat down. "It means a lot to my family that you have not forgotten us."

"These are very difficult days for you," I said.

"Yes, you're right. Life is not easy," Amal admitted. "I get tired of going to prison every day as well as looking after my family. But God is so good to us! Even if Ali never comes home alive, we will continue to praise the Lord, for we are in His will. We know that we have a wonderful future awaiting us in heaven, and we are so much looking forward to Jesus' return."

"You must be very strong."

"The Lord is our strength! He is taking care of us," she said as she smiled broadly. "Do you know that during the ten months that Ali has been in prison, I haven't once been sick for a single day?

God is using Ali, too—he has had so many opportunities to talk to people about Christ there in that prison."

Amal told me about one recent convert, a young man who had been sent away by his own family because he had become a Christian. His long search for the truth had ended when he spent a few days in prison. There he'd met Ali. Now he was a frequent visitor to Amal's home, calling her his "spiritual mother."

"God's ways are higher than our ways," Amal concluded. "And every one of us wants to be in the center of his will."

To my amazement, there in the sub-Saharan desert, I was treated to delicious coffee and something that reminded me of *oliebollen*—a special cookielike treat we have on New Year's Eve in Holland. Amal had sprinkled hers with grated coconut instead of our customary powdered sugar, but it couldn't have been more delicious.

## "I WILL NOT FORGET . . ."

We talked nonstop through my visit, and before long we were running out of time. Before we left I had to ask Amal just one more question—one that had been burning in my mind. "Amal, I heard that you were sentenced to twenty lashes. Please tell me what happened."

I was surprised when she began to laugh.

"Oh, that—" She chuckled. "That happened the third time Ali had to appear in court. I wanted to go inside the courtroom, but the guard wouldn't let me in. I knew it was my right to be present when my husband was accused, so I started to shout, telling the guard at the door what was on my mind. The judge heard the racket outside, and when he was told what it was all about, he ordered me to come in.

" 'Why are you shouting like that?' he demanded.

" 'Because they won't let me in, and it's my right to be here!' I answered.

"The judge knew I was right, but he had to retain his sense of authority. 'Shut up,' he ordered me, 'or I'll sentence you to prison, just like your husband. Then your children won't have anyone to care for them.'

"That infuriated me," Amal told me. "It made me so mad that I slammed my fist on his table. 'You're supposed to be a judge, making lawful judgments; this is unlawful!'"

Seeing that Amal would not give in, the judge sentenced her to twenty lashes on the spot. Amal looked at Ali, and he motioned to her that she had better give up the fight.

"I was ordered to kneel down on a sand pillow, but I refused," Amal recalled. "'If you want to beat me, beat me, but I will remain standing,' I told them."

As Amal recalled the story, a smile remained on her face. I couldn't understand it.

"But, Amal, didn't it hurt terribly?" I asked. "Didn't the skin of your back come off? Wasn't there a lot of pain the following days?"

"Oh no," she replied. "Do you know what happened? As I stood there, I closed my eyes and concentrated my thoughts on Jesus. I honestly didn't feel the camel's whip. And I saw Jesus. I saw him! And even during the days after the lashing, my back was not sore. That was the Lord's supernatural power. After the female police officer beat me, she took me aside and said she was sorry for what had happened because it was unfair.

"'It wasn't your fault,' I told her. 'You were just obeying orders.'

"'You know,' she remarked, 'a lot of people refuse to kneel down when they are lashed, but this is the first time I've ever seen anyone remain standing throughout the whole ordeal.'"

I was overcome by Amal's story. I couldn't have said another word even if I'd wanted to. Thankfully, at that very moment, the children offered to sing for me. The first song was in Arabic, but the second one I understood:

I've got a home in glory land that outshines the sun!
Do Lord, oh, do Lord, oh, do remember me. . . .

They repeated the words over and over again. As I listened, I heard the Lord's quiet voice speaking to my heart, saying, *Anneke, I do remember this family. I will never leave them nor forsake them.*

I couldn't resist embracing Amal as I left. I had no idea whether it was culturally correct to do so, and at a time like that I didn't really care. Our earthly cultures made no difference right then. All that mattered was the fact that we were sisters in Christ, members of the same worldwide family. It was hard for both of us to end our embrace, for although our time together had been short, our hearts had been joined together forever.

During the weeks that followed, Johan and I visited other African countries, but my thoughts often went back to Amal and never more so than during our final moments in Africa.

As we waited for our return flight at the Nairobi airport, we struck up a conversation with a lady from Austria. I had noticed her earlier because she looked so sad and seemed to be rather absent-minded. We were shocked when we heard what had happened to her. Two days before, she and her husband had been near the end of a five-week vacation. Near Mombasa they were enjoying the beach and the nearby safari parks.

Then suddenly, while snorkeling over a coral reef, her husband died of a heart attack.

Johan and I helped the Austrian woman find her way around the busy airport and onto her plane. We listened as she recalled the sad events of the last two days.

As our plane climbed high into the African skies, I kept seeing the faces of the two women—Amal and the Austrian widow. Amal's brightly shining eyes were full of hope and joy despite her difficult circumstances. The other lady's haunted eyes and devastated posture reflected her empty heart. Her only hope seemed to rest in the fact that her husband had been a good man who had paid his financial dues to the church where they belonged.

That morning I had read the words of Jesus in Mark 10:29-31:

> "I tell you the truth," Jesus replied, "no one who has left home or brothers or sisters or mother or father or children or fields for me and the gospel will fail to receive a hundred times as much in this present age (homes, brothers, sisters, mothers, children and fields—and with them, persecutions) and in the age to come, eternal life. But many who are first will be last, and the last first."

It is costing Amal and her family everything to follow Christ, but he is making it up to them—I saw that with my own eyes. He is making it up to them in this present age by giving them hope, new family members, and a house of their own—and, as he predicted, with persecution. And in the coming age they will have eternal life with him.

Like so many other persecuted Christians, Amal and her husband have chosen the best part. God is remembering them. As we pray for the wives and families of persecuted Christians around the world, so should we.

# Turning Periods into Commas

Remember those in prison as if you were their
fellow prisoners, and those who are mistreated
as if you yourselves were suffering.

*Hebrews 13:3*

About thirty years ago, I heard about the Suffering Church for the first time. Brother Andrew was the speaker, and he shared about his many travels behind the Iron Curtain—bringing Bibles and encouragement to Christians who were severely persecuted for their faith.

"I believe that in the measure we help them carry their burden, their weight gets lighter," Brother Andrew told us.

His words brought to mind one of my physics classes. Physics was far from my favorite subject in high school, but I knew what Andrew said was true in the natural world. If we have to move a heavy piece of furniture, and Johan and I work together—he may shoulder the majority of the load, but the weight I carry is deducted from his share of the burden.

The same kind of rule applies in the spiritual realm. And there are several ways in which we can lighten the burden of our suffering brothers and sisters. Let me share a few with you.

## THE POWER OF PRAYER

It may surprise you that I've put prayer on top of the list, but it is not by accident. In fact, prayer is the most important effort we can make. Perhaps you've noticed that prayer is often the first thing the apostle Paul asks for when he finishes his letters in the New Testament. He knows how strategic prayer is.

Whenever we ask persecuted Christians on our visits what we can do to help them, we get the same answer almost every time: "Please pray for us." Why? Because the Suffering Church understands the amazing power of prayer.

For seventy years Russian Christians prayed for their nation. They cried out to God faithfully and relentlessly. We in the West prayed, too. Only eternity will tell how the fervent prayers of persecuted Russian Christians, along with those of their brothers and sisters abroad, were instrumental in the political changes that dismantled the Soviet Union during the last decade of this century. I believe that the prayers of Christians paved the way for the fall of the Iron Curtain.

We don't always see the results of prayer from a distance; sometimes prayer affects our lives in a very personal way. Sometimes we find ourselves on the receiving end of prayer. When that happens, it makes us realize just how powerful prayer can be. Our own family experienced that during the days and weeks following July 11, 1995.

It was a beautiful summer evening, and we were having dinner in the garden after a busy day of painting the outside of our house. Suddenly the phone rang. One of our youngest son's friends was calling from the hospital. "Could you please come over immediately?" he said. "Martijn has had an accident. . . ."

The young man did not say how bad Martijn's injuries were, but the sound of his voice told me everything I needed to know. Our hearts pounding, Johan and I rushed to the hospital.

When we arrived, the look on the nurse's face did not promise anything good. She didn't have much to say. "The doctors have been running some tests," she explained, "and we'll all just have to wait and see."

As we sat in the waiting room, Martijn's friend told us what had happened. They had gone to the beach, and on the way home, Martijn was sitting in the back of a Chevy pickup. Coming off the beach, their vehicle passed under a large steel beam, meant to prevent trucks and campers from entering the beach area.

Just as they rode under the beam, Martijn stood up to catch a chair that was falling over. The side of his head hit the beam, and Martijn was knocked unconscious. Blood ran from his ears, and he started to vomit. He had been rushed to the hospital by ambulance.

About an hour after we arrived in the hospital, the neurologist told us the details of our son's condition. He had suffered brain damage from the severe blow to his head. Although the X rays did not show any hemorrhaging in his brain, if that were to happen during the coming days, it would make his condition critical. Even now his left side was paralyzed, and he was in a coma. "I can't really predict his future," the doctor told us, his expression grim. "Your son may completely recover, but there's also a very real possibility that he could die."

Once we were taken into Intensive Care to see Martijn, the truth sank in. Our tall, athletic sixteen-year-old was lying motionless in the fetal position. He did not react to our words or our touch. Blood was still dripping from his ears.

With our older two children, we surrounded his bed, held hands, and prayed. It was all we could do. In moments like that what a privilege it is to turn to the one who rules the universe. What a comfort it is to appeal to a loving heavenly Father, who knows about every detail of our lives. Even then, in the midst of everything, we somehow realized that God would always remain the same—loving, compassionate, good—no matter what the future held for Martijn.

We went home to shower and change and make a few phone calls. One call was to a family member, one to a church member, and one to an Open Doors colleague. Only three phone calls, but what a difference they made! They activated a vast prayer chain that stretched all around the world.

It wasn't long before we felt the result of those prayers.

How else could I explain the peace, passing all understanding, that filled our hearts? How else could we have experienced the goodness and love of the Lord at a time when we should have felt nothing but panic and soul-searching doubt?

During the days that followed, as I entered the hospital, I often thought, *I must be the most privileged person here. I wonder if any other patient's family has so many people praying for them?*

And God answered. Martijn recovered, and apart from a slight loss of hearing, he has not suffered any lasting effects of the accident.

For Johan and me, our son's terrible accident was an object

lesson in the power of prayer. If other people's prayers could have this effect on us, surely our prayers for others make a difference in other people's lives.

## PRAYER FOR THE SUFFERING CHURCH

In Hebrews 13:3 Paul tells us to remember the prisoners as if we were imprisoned with them. I can't think of a better way to feel a little of what the Suffering Church is going through than by identifying with them in prayer.

I loved visiting a dear elderly lady from our church when she was still alive. We called her "Moe [Mother] Schaap." Moe had a burden to pray. Her list of missionaries was very long. She not only prayed for persecuted Christians, she also cried a lot when she prayed.

As she grew older and was unable to walk or remember much of what she was reading, she developed a special way of prayer. She put prayer letters or news briefs on her lap and said, "Lord, I cannot remember all of this. Would you please come and sit beside me and read what's here." Then she would close her eyes and just sit there, trying to feel what the prisoners were feeling. God understood her tears and her sighs. She was an example to me of what it means to remember those who suffer "as if you yourselves were suffering." When we pray, God is not impressed by our eloquent words but by the humble condition of our hearts.

Prayer is at the vital center of our Open Doors ministry, and there are many resources available from the national Open Doors office that will inform you of current needs and guide you as to how you can pray for the Suffering Church. Please contact the Open Doors office for your country (listed in the back of this book), and ask them to send you their free monthly prayer calendar, which will give you a good overview of current needs.

Upon request, Open Doors also will send you a free prayer tape with current information and first-hand testimonies. Some people use these tapes to pray privately in their home. Others meet regularly with a group to pray.

"Partners in Prayer" is a network of prayer groups in the

United States and Canada committed to praying regularly and strategically for persecuted Christians. Each group consists of two or more people praying an hour or more every month. This prayer network has been formed to help encourage, empower, and equip the Suffering Church. Contact your national Open Doors office for more information or to receive a leader's application form.

Open Doors also can furnish you with a resource list that contains information on specific prayer campaigns, prayer groups, prayer conferences, prayer cards of individual persecuted believers, a telephone hot line to call for the latest and most urgent requests, and other prayer tools. (Please note that the list of available resources varies slightly from office to office.)

Our newsletters contain a prayer calendar, with one subject for prayer each day. These can be used in your devotions or for family prayers at the dinner table. You can also use them to motivate your pastor or other church members not to forget the persecuted Christians around the world in their prayers.

## STAYING INFORMED

To be able to pray specifically, we need to know who is suffering and where.

In this book I have only been able to share the stories of a few women who are paying a price for their faith. There a many, many more around the world. If you subscribe to our free newsletters, you will be informed on a regular basis about religious persecution around the world.

You can stay informed about the persecuted church by requesting a complimentary subscription to Open Doors *Newsbrief*. This monthly publication brings you the most up-to-date information available concerning Christians living in the world's most difficult areas. As you read it your faith will be built by learning of God's mighty works behind the enemy's lines. Most important, you'll learn how to touch the lives of your persecuted brothers and sisters, letting them know they are not forgotten. You can be part of the solution for those living where faith costs the most! Contact the appropriate national Open Doors office from the list in the back of this book to receive a complimentary subscription to *Newsbrief*.

Apart from Open Doors, there are other groups that share the same burden. Some of these include the World Evangelical Fellowship's Liberty Commission, Freedom House's Center for Religious Freedom, and the International World Day of Prayer for the Persecuted Church. These can be accessed through an Internet search.

Open Doors USA has launched a dynamic new Web site featuring "10 Things You Can Do to Get Involved" with the persecuted church. Included are resources to inform and equip you, teach you to pray and to advocate, allow you to go and to give, and much more. Click on www.opendoorsusa.org to do all this and more.

Another helpful resource is Compass Direct News Service. This service is dedicated to providing exclusive news, penetrating reports, moving interviews, and insightful analyses of situations and events facing Christians persecuted for their faith. Whether you are a media outlet, organization, church, or just a concerned individual, you'll find Compass Direct an invaluable resource with information presented in a way you can use it. For subscription information, call 949-862-0300, or E-mail them at compassdr@ compuserve.com.

*Frontline World Report* is a sixty-second daily radio news program featuring breaking news from the persecuted church. It is produced and distributed daily via satellite to radio stations across America. If you'd like to hear this program on your local station each day, contact the Open Doors USA office to obtain a demo CD of this program, which can then be given to your local Christian radio station manager.

## ADVOCACY FOR THE SUFFERING

One way to become involved is to be an "advocate" for suffering Christians around the world. An advocate, according to Webster's Dictionary, is someone who "pleads the cause of another; defends, vindicates, or espouses a case by argument, is friendly to; an upholder; a defender."

In some cases, political pressure can make a big difference. Writing letters to ambassadors, congressmen, presidents, and others in authority—these are all ways in which we can lighten the burden of those who are persecuted for their faith.

In the chapter about Rachel, you saw how political pressure in Washington contributed to the release of her husband, Wim, from a Saudi Arabian prison. In the Sudan the government has been reluctant to carry out the death sentence given to one particular Muslim-background believer for becoming a Christian. According to Sudanese law, such people should be executed. But because this brother was well known abroad, he was eventually released instead of killed. In several other instances, prisoners' treatment has been improved as soon as their cases were published in the West.

Since love is faith in action, Open Doors can provide you with tools to help you or your group put faith into action by advocating on behalf of suffering Christians. By visiting the Open Doors USA Web site at www.opendoorsusa.org, you'll learn how you can put your faith into action by writing letters to the editor of your local newspaper, sending an E-mail to your congressman, or writing a news release, among other options.

## KEEPING IN TOUCH

In the previous chapters you read of many instances where letters and cards from abroad greatly encouraged persecuted Christians. A few words from a child have shed light in darkness. Letters and cards show that, though isolated, a person is not forgotten. It reminds those who suffer that other members of the body of Christ care about their situation. Our Open Doors offices have updated lists available of these people's names and addresses. The information you receive will also inform you about what you can say in your letters without causing problems for the persons to whom you write.

Each year there are a variety of opportunities for you to encourage and strengthen believers in person. China, Vietnam, Latin America, and the Middle East are some of the areas where individuals can visit the work of Open Doors on the front lines. All travel is subject to current local conditions and the degree of danger to the Christians living in restricted areas.

Open Doors also brings the Suffering Church to you as part of our regional conferences, held in two or three American cities annually. These conferences provide in-depth information on our work and the most current news from behind the front lines. Our speakers are men and women who actually work in the field and have an intimate knowledge of the plight of believers in their respective regions. We also provide opportunities for you to meet and hear reports from members of the persecuted church at our regional meetings when it can be arranged.

Many Christians are still ignorant of the plight of their brothers and sisters in other parts of the world. You can play a role in creating awareness for the Suffering Church. You can support the International Day of Prayer and help organize special meetings to pray for the persecuted church. You can help make arrangements to invite a speaker to come and share in your area about the subject. There are good audiovisual aids available to help you show others what price some people pay for their faith. Contact the organizations mentioned below to help you get started. Many more volunteers are needed to help spread the word.

## COMMAS INSTEAD OF PERIODS

My husband, Johan, likes to speak on Acts 14 when he challenges Christians around the world to care for the Suffering Church.

In that chapter we read how the authorities won over the crowd over and stoned Paul. They dragged him out of the city, thinking he was dead.

"*Period!*" Johan tells his audience. "The devil wanted to put a period here. Paul was finished as far as the enemy was concerned. But God had other plans. The story continues, 'But after the disciples had gathered around him, he got up and went back into the city' (Acts 14:20). Something happened that turned the devil's period into God's comma. What made the difference? The disciples' prayers."

God loves to change the devil's periods into commas, and he's still doing it today.

It is my heart's desire that he will use you and me to make a difference in the lives of Christians who are persecuted for their faith around the world. We can reach out to them, each in our own church and community and in our own way, through awareness, through action, and most of all, through prayer.

# By Brother Andrew

*Taste and see that the Lord is good;*
*blessed is the man who takes refuge in him.*
*Psalm 34:8*

More than thirty years ago I was introduced to a vibrant young Dutchman named Johan Companjen. Although he made a very good impression on me at the time, I never could have imagined that this enthusiastic student would one day be given responsibility for the entire operation of Open Doors International.

In late 1968, on his first mission abroad for our ministry, Johan traveled to Vietnam to serve as a technician. His fiancée, Anneke, had already begun a teaching job and had to stay behind in Holland. I can still remember how heavy Anneke's heart was as she said good-bye to the man she planned to marry.

Shortly before Johan's departure, we held a "farewell meeting," as we called it, to send Johan off with our love, our prayers, and our blessings. Our dear friend Corrie ten Boom was present as well. At the end of the evening, Corrie went up to Johan, took his hand in hers, and said something that he still treasures today:

"Johan, I'm so glad you're going. Vietnam is a good place, in spite of the war. Don't worry if people say you're crazy to be going to such a dangerous place. Remember that the best place for you to be is in the center of God's will. And if that is Vietnam, then you're better off living in Vietnam than staying home in Holland. The most dangerous place in the world's eyes is actually the safest place you can possible be—if God puts you there."

Corrie didn't mean, of course, that God automatically protects us from danger or that nothing bad will ever happen to us. Rather, she meant that God is with us at all times, using everything that *does* happen to us to accomplish his good purposes. Our job is to listen to his prompting and to follow wherever he leads.

Clearly, Johan was following Jesus that day. But although Anneke agreed with his decision, as she and I watched the plane that carried Johan take off from Amsterdam airport, she was trying very hard not to cry. Those were treacherous days in Vietnam, and she couldn't help but wonder whether she would ever see him again. She didn't weep until he was out of sight, and then her tears spilled freely. It would be the first of many, many separations the two of them would experience for the sake of the gospel. And it was Anneke's first encounter with the heartache of separation from Johan, a heartache that has given her a deep understanding of the struggles of other women around the world who pay the price for their Christian faith.

Once Johan returned from Vietnam, I was privileged to conduct the wedding ceremony that united him and Anneke in marriage. Since then, Johan and I have worked side-by-side for nearly twenty-five years, and Johan is now president of Open Doors, International. In all the years I have known them, it has been always evident to me that Johan and Anneke both listen to and follow their Savior's voice.

I watched as the Companjen's three children grew up and left home. I rejoiced with Anneke when she was able to join Johan in his travels. And I saw her heart increasingly moved with compassion for the women she has written about in this book—women who are often forgotten in their hidden sorrow.

It is both interesting and fitting that Corrie ten Boom was present when Johan and Anneke first began their lives together in God's service, because the women Anneke has written about have much in common with Corrie. As with them, it was suffering that brought Corrie to the place where God could best use her. We might never have heard of Corrie had she not spent time in a concentration camp. Her suffering—and the way she dealt with it—has set an example for women and men throughout the world who are faced with injustice, persecution, and pain.

Like the women you've just read about, Corrie was a woman of prayer. I can still remember her bold approach to intercession. Sometimes she would open the Bible during a prayer time, lift it toward heaven, and say, "Look! See what it says right here? That's a promise, Lord. And you have to keep your promises!"

As is the case with the women in the book, Corrie was often isolated and cut off from all Christian support. She had no one to rely on but God, and nowhere to turn but to him. She was courageous in her confidence and liked to remind everyone who knew her, "We are hidden in Christ," and folding one hand over the other, she would add with a smile, "in God." As she told Johan, her sense of safety and belonging was utterly reliant on being at the center of God's will.

Corrie, like most of the women Anneke has written about, had much to forgive. Her story of forgiving the Nazi captor who was responsible for her sister Betsie's death is a familiar one. Not so well known is the struggle she had in forgiving a group of fellow Christians who kicked her out of a battered women's shelter—a project she had personally founded and funded herself.

Perhaps the greatest lesson any of us learned from Corrie was one she was taught in her "Bible school"—Ravensbruck concentration camp. It was there that she came to terms with the fact that God is unfailingly good, even when life is very, very bad.

One day after Corrie had settled in California, I was walking with her through the lovely garden that graced the back of her house. Her garden was filled with every kind of flower imaginable, and on that lovely sunny day I could hardly contain my joy in the Lord.

"Ah, God is good, Corrie," I exulted, inhaling the fragrant air.

It was the only time in all the years of our friendship that I heard a note of rebuke in her words to me. Her mind had immediately flashed back to her sister's tragic death at Ravensbruck.

"Yes, Andrew. But God was also good when Betsie died."

Corrie ten Boom never wanted anyone to forget that God's nature never changes, no matter how terrible the circumstances may be. If she could have met and ministered to the faithful women we've met in the pages of this book, she would have encouraged them in their prayers, assured them of their refuge in Christ, and urged them to forgive. But I think, above all else, she would have reminded them that even though the way is dark and difficult, and even though the price they have paid for their faith is enormous, our Lord's nature is unchanging.

Even today I can almost hear her saying it: *"God is good!"*

# APPENDIX

For more information visit our Web site at www.opendoors.org
or write:

AUSTRALIA . . . . . . Open Doors Australia
P.O. Box 53
Seaforth
NSW, 2092
Australia

BRAZIL . . . . . . . . Portas Abertas
CP 45371
Vila Mariana
CEP 04010-970
Sao Paulo
Brazil

CANADA. . . . . . . . Open Doors
P.O. Box 597
Streetsville, ON
L5M 2CI
Canada

DENMARK. . . . . . . Abne Dore
P.O. Box 171
DK-6900 Skjern
Denmark

FRANCE . . . . . . . . Portes Ouvertes
BP 139
F-67833 Tanneries Cedex
France

GERMANY. . . . . . . Offene Grenzen
Postfach 2010
D-38718 Seesen
Germany

ITALY . . . . . . . . Porte Aperte
Casa Postale 45
37063 Isola Della Scala, VR
Italy

KOREA . . . . . . . Open Doors
Hyerim Presbyterian Church
Street No. 403
Sungne 3-dong
Kangdong-gu #134-033
Seoul
Korea

NETHERLANDS . . . . Open Doors
Postbus 47
3850 AA Ermelo
The Netherlands

NEW ZEALAND . . . . Open Doors
P.O. Box 27-630
Mt Roskill
Auckland 1030
New Zealand

NORWAY . . . . . . . Åpne Dører
Boks 4698 Grim
N-4673 Kristiansand
Norway

PHILIPPINES . . . . . Open Doors
P.O. Box 1573-1155
QCCPO Main
1100 Quezon City
Philippines

SINGAPORE . . . . . . Open Doors
150 Orchard Road
#08-20 Orchard Road
Singapore 238841

SOUTH AFRICA. . . . Open Doors
Box 990099
Kibler Park 2053
Johannesburg
South Africa

SPAIN . . . . . . . . Puertas Abiertas
Apartado 578
28850 Torrejon de Ardoz
Madrid
Spain

SWITZERLAND . . . . Portes Ouvertes
Case Postale 267
CH-1008 Prilly
Lausanne
Switzerland

UNITED KINGDOM . . Open Doors
P.O. Box 6
Witney
Oxon OX8 7SP
United Kingdom

UNITED STATES . . . Open Doors
P.O. Box 27001
Santa Ana, CA 92799
USA
E-mail: usa@opendoors.org